STEALTH AIRCRAFT

BILL SWEETMAN

Publishers & Wholesalers Inc.
Osceola, Wisconsin 54020, USA   ®

For Martin

Acknowledgements

There are many people—far too many to list—who have spared time over the past ten years to brief me on many different programs, and I owe them the background knowledge of aerospace technology which forms the basis of this book. A vote of thanks to all of them.

Particular thanks for help, ideas, mental stimulation and encouragement are due to Jerry Cantwell, Dave Smith, Jim Goodall, Lee M. Graham, Mike Badrocke, John Andrews and Jay Miller. A special word goes to Dave Arnold of Motorbooks International, who convinced me that the project was feasible.

First published in 1986 by Motorbooks International Publishers & Wholesalers Inc., PO Box 2, 729 Prospect Avenue, Osceola, Wisconsin 54020, USA

© Bill Sweetman 1986

Library of Congress Cataloging-in-Publication Data
Sweetman, Bill.
    Stealth aircraft, secrets of future airpower.

    1. Stealth aircraft.   I. Title.
UG1240.S953   1986   358.4'183   85-25844
ISBN 0-87938-208-2 (soft)

Printed and bound in the United States of America

Motorbooks International books are also available at discounts in bulk quantity for industrial or sales-promotional use. For details write to the marketing manager at the publisher's address

Cover illustration by Jefrey Gunion, Ben Lomond, CA.

Contents

Introduction

Stealth is a highly classified area of military development. Writing a book on the subject is a challenge, calling for the use of analysis, deduction and straightforward reporting.

In the case of many classified programs, it is possible to trace references back to a time when the subject was not considered important enough to be classified, and to uncover unclassified reports and papers which at least tell part of the story. Stealth, however, originated in the reconnaissance community, where secrecy is a way of life, and it was brought to maturity in the windowless Lockheed Skunk Works. To my knowledge, not one technical paper dealing specifically with Stealth has been published, nor has a single unclassified briefing on Stealth been given, on or off the record.

None of the information in the following pages has been obtained from classified sources. A writer needs classified data like a fish needs a bicycle. Not only is it unusable, but if it confirms a point which has been deduced or obtained elsewhere it may become impossible to use the legitimately obtained information.

Some of the material in this book is drawn directly from open sources: technical papers, textbooks, catalogs, trade journals and unclassified briefings. In some cases a single data point, isolated in one publication, proved most significant when it filled a gap in a larger pattern.

A few pieces of information in this book, such as the shapes of the principal Stealth aircraft under development, are based on unconfirmed reports, published and otherwise. Where this is the case, I have said as much in the text.

Most of the book, though, is based on a first-principles analysis of the problems and opportunities involved in making a large vehicle vanish into thin air—at least as far as any feasible sensor system is concerned. While specific details of Stealth aircraft may be secret, the conditions which govern their design—the threat, the properties of radar waves or the principles of aerodynamics—are not, and this makes such an analysis possible.

Omissions and misplaced emphases are inevitable when one writer attempts to guess the results of a decade's work by thousands of experienced engineers. I can predict with complete confidence that some of these will be revealed over the next few years, as details of these new aircraft are released. Meanwhile, the mystery which surrounds this major technical achievement can only add to its fascination.

Bill Sweetman
November 1985

CHAPTER 1

Now you see it ...

Burbank, California, is not among the world's architectural treasures. The predominant tone in the cityscape is a sandy beige, and the biggest blocks of that uninspiring color are the massive hangars of the Lockheed-California Company, one of two aircraft-building arms of the Lockheed Corporation. About 15,000 people worked for Lockheed-California at Burbank in early 1985, and the company was recruiting aggressively. It is hard to assess how many other people worked for the dozens of small engineering firms that cluster around Lockheed's Burbank plant, like remora fish that pick up the tidbits left by a shark, but the number must have been substantial.

The floor space and workforce at the Lockheed plant alone put it among the United States' bigger aircraft manufacturing plants. It compares roughly with the General Dynamics facility at Fort Worth, which turns out fifteen F-16 fighters each month. But—as far as the public record goes—Burbank does next to nothing. It produces some subassemblies for Lockheed's P-3 patrol aircraft, but the type is actually built at Palmdale, fifty miles to the north. The TR-1/U-2 reconnaissance aircraft is also built at Palmdale, and the S-3B antisubmarine warfare type will be produced alongside the P-3.

The answer to the puzzle is not hard to find, although no spokesman for Lockheed or the Pentagon will provide it. By far the greatest part of Lockheed-California's activity centers on military programs which are so highly classified that the names, shapes and missions of the aircraft involved are secret. Security barriers exist even between those working on such a program; access to any information requires a positive "need-to-know" status. All activity takes place in windowless, security-screened buildings, from which even senior executives and United States Air Force (USAF) officers are barred unless they have a role in the development effort. The industry and the Pentagon call these programs "black."

Lockheed-California has been involved in black programs for more than three decades, but never as much as it is now. Neither is Lockheed the only aircraft manufacturer to be heavily involved in secret work. Northrop Corporation is on its way to becoming the largest defense contractor in the United States, some pundits believe, largely because of its work on a program called the Advanced Technology Bomber (ATB). Unclassified material on the ATB amounts to a couple of dozen words. General Dynamics' San Diego division is developing a new cruise missile for the USAF, again in complete secrecy.

The common thread connecting all these programs—and, almost certainly, other and even better concealed efforts—is Stealth. The purpose of this book is to provide answers, from unclassified sources, to the basic questions about Stealth: What is it? Why is it important? Why, if it is so important, was it not developed earlier? How does it work, and how well?

What is Stealth? The term was first introduced into public discussion in 1980, having been heard in military aviation circles for several years. By 1982, however, the subject had become so sensitive that company, government and USAF people were prohibited from even using the word "Stealth" in any official, unclassified context.

This secrecy is excessive. Stealth is not some completely new technology, the smallest hint of which must be kept from a potential adversary. Rather, it is a quality of a weapon system, like war load, range or speed. Some publicly revealed and unclassified systems are already Stealthy, to some degree. The new "black" programs are mostly different in that Stealth is a more important, and in some cases the most important, quality of the aircraft.

The purpose of Stealth is to improve the ability of a weapon system to carry out its mission, by making it more difficult to detect. In some cases, Stealth is intended to delay detection and to lessen the opponent's ability to track the target's course after detection. In the case of a true Stealth aircraft, the goal is to achieve such a high level of Stealth that the system will probably perform its mission without being detected at all.

The important word here is *probably*. There is no such thing as an invisible aircraft. But neither is there certainty in a military operation. If the probability of detection is reduced, the chances that the vehicle will survive and complete its mission are accordingly increased.

When Stealth becomes an important quality of a system, or even its single most important quality, it affects every aspect of the design that can be observed from a distance. This means not only the entire shape of the aircraft, but also its own emissions of heat and electrical radiation. In the case of a highly Stealthy aircraft, "observables" and related issues dominate the design the way that speed-related issues dominate the design of a Mach 3 aircraft.

In the eighties and nineties, in the view of many experts, Stealth has become attainable, and is quickly becoming necessary; it is an idea whose time has come. The best way of understanding this opinion is through a review of some of the long-term trends in air combat—long-term meaning the entire history of air warfare.

This book is mainly about aircraft and missiles, but Stealth can be a consideration in the design of other weapons. Ship and tank designs can benefit from an analysis of why they are detectable, and what can be done to reduce the risks of detection. In fact, one entire branch of military science has been dominated by Stealth since its inception: submarine warfare. Avoiding detection, mainly by reducing submerged noise, but partly through designing sonar-resistant hulls and using anechoic (anti-echo) coatings, has been, and remains, one of the main thrusts of submarine design.

For submarine warfare, this was a natural development, since the main reason for building a submersible warship in the first place was to avoid detection. Air warfare was different. Flight performance—speed, range and maneuverability—and firepower were considered to be the most important attributes of the military aircraft, from the first air combats over France in World War I to the Vietnam era.

Fighter pilots knew better. The pilots who gained the highest scores, in World War I, World War II and in the jet age, did not relish close-in combat and high-energy tail chases. Such actions gave the opponent a chance to escape, and there was always the danger of intervention by a second adversary. The top-scoring aces had no time for gallantry. They stressed the importance of seeing their opponent first and, ideally, completing the attack without being detected. In the classic attack, a pilot would see a target and quickly maneuver into the universal blindspot—silhouetted against the sun—before diving on the enemy.

The year 1917 saw some unique experiments in Germany, representing an attempt to put these combat lessons to use. At least two aircraft—a Fokker E.1 fighter and a Gotha bomber—were covered with heavy cellophane skins in an attempt to make them less visible. The experiment was not a success. Whether these original Stealth aircraft were harder to detect than the fabric-covered versions is not known, but the cellophane proved unequal to air loads and the environment. The appearance of the aircraft was probably more spectral than stealthy, with the wooden skeleton visible through the skin; its main effect on the enemy might have been psychological.

Otherwise, observability was largely neglected, partly because air warfare had its

A heavy bomber like the B-52G is a powerful weapon. It is also a very large target for radar and other sensors, weighing more than 200 tons fully loaded. (Boeing)

cultural roots in naval and ground combat. In both environments, it could usually be assumed that opposing forces would see each other at the same time, or as near as made no difference, and this philosophy was unconsciously brought over to air power. The only concession to observability was the use of camouflage, but even that was not always applied consistently or scientifically.

Neither did anyone in high places ever connect high bomber loss rates in World War II with the increasing size of strategic bombers and the constant size of interceptors. Another interesting case is that of the twin-engined, "destroyer" fighter, the darling of the pre-1939 theoreticians, which in operational service proved generally unsuitable for day-fighter operations. The only exception was the Lockheed P-38 Lightning, which by virtue of its unusual configuration had much smaller side and front profiles than any other operational twin. The P-38 may, in fact, have been the first aircraft in which design for reduced observability was operationally significant.

One reason not much was done about detectability was that in the formative years of air warfare there was a limit to what could be done. Up to the late thirties, the only target acquisition and identification device in service was the unaided human eye. The eye is limited in range, but its resolution (its ability to distinguish detail) is extremely high, and it is difficult to fool. The only practical way to delay optical detection is to make the target smaller in linear dimensions (which are what the eye sees). Because dimensions do not vary directly with weight, a very substantial reduction in the weight of the target would be needed to make any significant impact on visibility. This was tried with a number of lightweight fighters, such as the French Caudron series, but the penalties in speed, range, armament and armor were generally unacceptable and the benefits were small.

By the thirties, the speeds and altitudes of modern aircraft were beginning to reach the point where air warfare changed dramatically. Advanced technology—metal airframes, supercharging and pressure cabins—made it possible for bombers to fly out of earshot from the ground and arrive over the target undetected. Because of increasing speeds and altitudes, the volume of sky to be searched by the fighter pilot increased, to the point where unaided visual interception of a large bomber force became impossible.

Another technical innovation restored the balance between the attack and the defense. Radar gave enough warning to launch fighters against fast bombers, to determine the bearing of an attack and to assess raid strength beyond visual range. The first early-warning radars were introduced in the late thirties, and air combat was never the same again.

One vital fact was soon recognized: While air defense had been greatly reinforced by radar, it was also becoming entirely dependent on it, for two reasons. One was that speeds and altitudes had outrun the capability of the human eye; the other was that electronic aids developed in parallel with radar and, later, radar itself made it possible for the attacker to strike accurately at night or in bad weather.

It was also quickly discovered that a radar device or radio beacon, unlike any previous weapon, did not need to be destroyed or physically damaged to be rendered ineffective. If its signals could be counterfeited, distorted or muffled with electronic noise, it could be neutralized just as effectively, often from a considerable distance. Electronic warfare (EW) had arrived.

The development of radar and EW technology was explosive. By 1945, ground-based radars ranged from transportable gun-laying sets to long-range early-warning systems with ranges of hundreds of miles. Experiments with airborne early-warning radar had started. Bombers carried target-mapping and navigation systems, and tail-warning radars, while fairly reliable, long-range radar was standard for heavy fighters, and was steadily being developed to give better, more accurate information to its operators. The day when a pilot could destroy a target without seeing it was not far off.

The changes in air warfare accelerated in the succeeding fifteen years. The jet engine opened new horizons in power and speed, and aircraft performance reached a point where—even with guidance from a ground radar—a successful engagement without the use of airborne radar was virtually impossible. The USAF took delivery of its last day fighter, with no search radar, in 1958; the Soviet armed forces passed the same milestone in the period 1963-64. The development of radar-guided surface-to-air

The most conspicuous aircraft in the world is probably the Soviet Union's Tupolev Tu-95 Bear bomber and reconnaissance aircraft. Its huge eight-bladed propellers cause a very distinctive radar echo; future Bear developments may have newly developed nonmetallic composite propellers. (US Navy)

missiles (SAMs) and air-to-air missiles (AAMs) had started in the period 1944-45, and after many years of work yielded practical systems in the mid- to late fifties. Guns were deleted from most fighters.

In the sixties, radar-guided weapons proliferated, in the shape of transportable and mobile SAMs and longer-range AAMs. Radome size became a key figure in fighter design: The standard to match was the thirty-six-inch radar dish of the F-4 Phantom, unquestionably the pre-eminent all-round combat aircraft of its day. The need for high speed, long range and maneuverability, together with the weight of the radar, missile armament and all-weather navigation systems, increased the weight of the USAF fighter by a factor of six between 1944 and 1964.

The growth of the fighter was matched by the growth of the bomber. The first major change was geopolitical. Superpower confrontation meant that future strategic bombing missions would be 8,000-10,000 miles long, including a return flight—three or four times the range of a B-29. Jet speed was also considered essential for survival, but jets were less efficient than pistons. The result was that strategic bombers grew by the mid-fifties into 200-ton aircraft, four times as big as a B-29.

A few people pointed out that this uncontrolled increase in aircraft size was not entirely a good thing. The big aircraft were not only expensive, but they were bigger

The jet age brought a phenomenal growth in aircraft size and observability. The Republic P-47 Thunderbolt was considered a monster in its day (this is the high-speed XP-47J prototype). (Smithsonian Institution/USAF)

targets and, other things being equal, could be picked up on radar at a greater range. As each new, bigger and faster generation of aircraft entered service, its greater speed was partly offset by the increased effective range of every hostile radar-controlled weapon deployed against it, so radar warning times tended to stay constant.

Nobody paid much attention to this argument. Instead, the emphasis was on defeating radar-guided weapons through tactics and jamming. The latter was becoming much more sophisticated, with the development of deception techniques: Instead of broadcasting noise, which would have made it clear that the signal was being jammed, the deception jammer subtly modified and retransmitted the radar signal.

Large aircraft not only carried jammers, but also pilotless decoy aircraft such as the Quail, launched from the B-52. The fielding of the Quail was an event of some significance to our story. The little drone was designed so that it generated a radar return similar to that of the 100-times-larger bomber, and thus demonstrated two vital points (the full importance of which was not immediately appreciated). One, the radar image of an aircraft was not necessarily proportional to its physical size. Two, air-

The XP-47J would have been dwarfed by the Convair YF-102 (shown here), which appeared ten years later. (Smithsonian Institution/USAF)

defense systems were now totally based on radar, and were vulnerable to any countermeasure based on this phenomenon.

However, most operators continued to rely on jamming and on tactics to foil radar. The most important tactical development, adopted in the late fifties and early sixties, was to make the attack run at low altitude. Most radar systems cannot see beyond the horizon, so if the target is below 500 feet, for example, it is invisible until it is thirty miles from the radar site. Airborne radars are not subject to the same range limitation, but the radars of the early sixties could not pick a target out at low altitude because of the strong reflections from the ground. Other tactical tricks included flying formations with one aircraft trailing the other, and slightly to its left or right; a hostile radar, even in its narrow-beam "tracking" mode, would have both targets in its beam at the same time, and it would be unable to get an accurate range on either.

The radar designers countered with improved systems of their own. Monopulse radars, which determine target position from a single, four-lobed pulse of energy rather than successive shots from a single beam, are harder to jam than their predecessors. New processing technology, using first analog and then digital computers, has made radars capable of transmitting a wider variety of waveforms, and of reading more information from a weak, jammed or distorted return. New power sources, such as the gridded traveling-wave tube developed in the sixties, have made it possible to achieve much higher peak power, so that the real echo from the target "burns through" the weaker signal from the jammer. In the late fifties, work started on pulse-Doppler radars, which detect the shift in echo frequency caused by the target's movement and can pick out low-flying targets against the ground.

EW theory was translated into practice over North Vietnam. The first US raids on North Vietnam, in early 1965, met with little opposition. In July of that year, however, the first emissions from an SA-2 missile radar were detected. Between that time and the suspension of bombing in 1969, the electronic conflict was intensive and dynamic. The 1972 Linebacker raids around Hanoi and Haiphong were on an even larger scale, and involved an EW effort of proportions which had not been contemplated before 1965.

A Linebacker strike could include seventy aircraft, of which only a minority carried offensive weapons. The balance of the force included fighter escorts and aircraft dedicated to EW. These included bombers carrying nothing but chaff (strands of metalized fiberglass, resembling a poor-quality blond wig), which created false echoes on the defensive radar screens. The chaff escorts had a dangerous job, because they naturally flew in front of this electronic smoke screen. Other support aircraft included B-66 bombers, laden with high-powered jamming equipment, and Wild Weasel aircraft, fitted with specially developed passive homing systems and loaded with missiles which homed in on hostile radars. Every aircraft which could do so carried its own jamming pod.

Other vital support missions were flown by manned and unmanned reconnaissance aircraft. Successful EW demands detailed knowledge of the workings of the defensive system, obtained by intercepting and analyzing all kinds of signals. Signals intelligence (SIGINT) is an enormous military activity in itself, and is hazardous even in peacetime, because it often involves provocative flights close to hostile airspace. (The

Royal Air Force calls such missions "ringing the fire alarm"; the purpose is to trigger an alert and record the response.) The Linebacker missions were successful, in terms of both results and loss rates. The immense resources devoted to EW, however, could hardly pass unnoticed, and neither could the magnitude of the risks involved in such tasks as SIGINT and chaff bombing. It was recognized, too, that the electronic battle had been close-run, and that the most modern Soviet missiles had not been deployed. It would not have taken a quantum leap in technology to shift the battle decisively against the attacker, and the USAF knew it.

It was at just that time that studies of a radical approach to the problem of EW began to become serious. What if it were possible to attack the EW problem at the source, by sharply reversing the trend of increasing detectability? Quite a lot of work in this area had already been done long before the Linebacker strikes, and those operations had indirectly benefited from it through improved intelligence. These proto-Stealth programs had proceeded quietly, and often without a great deal of funding, but they had laid the foundations for a radical change in the radar war.

The McDonnell GAM-72 (later, ADM-20) Quail was the first weapon to exploit the fact that a radar sees RCS, not physical size. To a radar, it appeared to be as large as a B-52. (McDonnell Douglas)

CHAPTER 2

Stealth in the sixties

The first serious attempts to make military aircraft less detectable, discounting the cellophane Fokker of 1917, were made by the US reconnaissance and intelligence community in the fifties. This is not the place to review the history of strategic reconnaissance, except to note that unauthorized entry into the airspace of another country was banned by international law and could be prevented by force if no other means was available. However, the British military intelligence organization sponsored covert flights over Germany in the late thirties, because the expansion of the German armed forces and weapons industry was taking place in unprecedented secrecy, and the traditional means of gathering intelligence, through military attachés, was no longer adequate.

The same situation, on a larger scale, confronted the United States after 1945, and the same solution was adopted. Converted bombers were used at first, but these were too vulnerable for operations over central Soviet Union, where most of the important military developments and production took place.

Late in 1952, USAF Major John Seaberg, a professional aeronautical engineer, started work on a design concept for an aircraft intended to plug the reconnaissance gap. It would combine a new-generation turbojet with a low-airspeed, high-altitude airframe, and would be capable of cruising at 70,000 feet. This was some miles higher than the world's absolute altitude record, set by a fighter in an all-out climb which ended when the aircraft ran out of airspeed. In March 1953, a specification was drafted for such an aircraft, including the requirement that "consideration will be given . . . to minimize the detectability by enemy radar." The standard for detectability had been devised by radar engineers, to compare and measure the performance of their systems. It was called "radar cross-section," or RCS. (It will be discussed in the next chapter.)

This requirement for reduced RCS was logical. The aircraft would operate alone at high altitude, and at that time no aircraft smaller than a medium bomber could hope to carry its own active jamming equipment. Avoiding observation would be ideal, although altitude was to be the primary defense.

There was another good reason for requiring reduced RCS. Intelligence is most valuable when the subject is unaware that it has been obtained. It is the work of minutes to push a secret prototype back into its hangar, and the work of seconds to shut down a sensitive transmission, so the quality of intelligence gathered by any system depends to some extent on its detectability.

Lockheed's U-2 was inspired by a requirement that emphasized minimum detectability. This was mainly achieved by meeting the performance and payload targets with a relatively small airframe, no larger than a contemporary fighter. (Lockheed)

"Radar's eye view" of the developed U-2R emphasizes the type's slender profile. The black paint is believed to possess some radar-absorbent qualities. (Lockheed)

As it happened, the USAF requirement was met indirectly. The "official" program, the Bell X-16, was the victim of an end run by Lockheed's chief engineer, Clarence L. "Kelly" Johnson. His belief, backed up by results on the P-80 and F-104 fighters, was that advanced aircraft should be designed and built by small teams of hand-picked people, working to meet a mission statement rather than a specification. An organization known as Advanced Development Projects (ADP) was set up along these lines at Burbank.

The small size of the ADP operation made it possible to achieve a very high degree of secrecy, something which also isolated the team from outside interference. Those without the need and clearance to know were barred from the ADP office and prototype shop, with ruthless impartiality. Lockheed people began to call it the Skunk Works, after the moonshine factory in the L'il Abner comic strip, and the name stuck despite high-level disapproval.

Johnson and the ADP joined forces with the Central Intelligence Agency (CIA) to provide a high-altitude reconnaissance aircraft. Project Aquatone started in November 1954, and was so secret that the aircraft did not even have a name when it made its first flight on August 1 the following year. It was designated U-2 soon afterward.

Reduced observables were a vital consideration in the design of the Lockheed A-12 family, of which the SR-71 shown here was the final development. Apparent in this view are the inward-canted fins, the wing-body blending and the outboard-mounted engines. (Lockheed)

Details of the SR-71 include the care with which abrupt discontinuities were eliminated from the shape and the use of chines to present an oblique surface to incoming radar signals. (Lockheed)

The U-2 proved highly successful. Its flight performance was outstanding, and although performance rather than RCS was the main driver in the design, the fact that it was a fighter-sized aircraft from most angles was probably important. It was barely half the weight of the USAF's X-16, which was canceled late in 1955. While studies were made of ways to reduce the radar image of the U-2, these are not believed to have gone further than the drawing board. The basic problem was that the U-2 was highly sensitive to extra weight and drag, and the benefit of any modification would have been offset by reduced performance.

From the start of the program, it was accepted that the U-2 would not be able to penetrate Soviet airspace indefinitely. Bigger radars and bigger SAMs would eventually be able to destroy the aircraft. Nobody knew exactly when this would happen (this was the sort of information that the U-2 was intended to gather), but studies of a U-2 replacement started as soon as the aircraft made its first operational flight over the Soviet Union, in July 1956.

The first effort involved a massive hydrogen-fueled aircraft, the L-400. It was abandoned for many sound reasons, but one look at its design confirms that it would have been a huge radar target compared to the U-2. After this false start, a completely fresh approach was made. This time, reduced detectability was a much higher priority than it had been in the design of the U-2.

This Ryan Q-2C drone was equipped with RAM blankets (the dark areas on the fuselage) and a wire-mesh fairing over the nose inlet. The fine mesh blocked radar waves out of the inlet duct. These modified drones proved almost impossible to track using contemporary fighter radars. (Teledyne Ryan Aeronautical)

This was necessary because the replacement system was to offer very high supersonic speed—as close to Mach 4 as possible—and this almost inevitably meant that it would be much bigger than the U-2. Unless the RCS was kept under control, the benefits of higher performance would be partly offset by the greater range at which hostile radars could detect and track the target.

Two companies made serious proposals to the CIA, which was managing the project with the help of the US Air Force. General Dynamics proposed a small aircraft to be launched in flight from a modified B-58; it was known in different versions as Fish and Kingfish, and would have been powered by a pure ramjet engine. At least one of the Fish/Kingfish studies featured a two-stage vehicle. The penetrator element made extensive use of radar-transparent, heat-resistant ceramics in its construction.

Lockheed's response was almost conservative in comparison to that of General Dynamics: a conventional delta-winged aircraft about the size of a B-58, with two turbo-ramjet engines—powerplants based on conventional turbojets, but integrated with complex inlet, bypass and nozzle systems so that they took on the characteristics of a ramjet at high speeds. It was this aircraft that was selected for development, under the code name Oxcart, in August 1959.

The performance goals for the new aircraft were as far ahead of most previous work as those of the U-2 had been: Low RCS was vital, but it had to be achieved without reducing performance. The only way to do this was to address the issue from the start of design work through the basic configuration. The shape of the Project Oxcart aircraft (later known as the A-12, and the progenitor of the SR-71) is familiar now, so much so

By 1967, the modified Q-2 had become the Model 147T, making extensive use of built-in RAM, rather than heavy blankets, to defeat radar. This photo, taken in Ryan's facility, shows a 147T development article which was used specifically to measure RCS. Evidence of the use of RAM and surface treatments is seen in the dark areas of the wing, nose and tail, and in the large wing fillets which give some of the advantages of wing-body blending. (Teledyne Ryan Aeronautical)

that it is helpful to look at it in detail and see how much the need for reduced observables affected the design.

The A-12 was very much the same size as a design of similar performance, the North American F-108 Rapier long-range interceptor, which was canceled a month after the A-12 was ordered. The final Rapier design had a jagged shape, with three large vertical fins, air intakes shaped like vertical wedges, and a deep slab-sided forebody carrying foreplanes. The main fuselage was a long, square-sectioned box containing the engines, fuel and weapons, with shoulder-mounted wings.

The A-12 was startlingly different. The aircraft's engines were in separate nacelles, at mid-span on the wing. The engines had conical, axisymmetrical inlets. The fuselage was much longer than the Rapier's, and very slender, being basically sized by the cockpit cross-section. The wing ran through the fuselage and nacelles at mid-height. (Viewed from the front, Johnson said, the aircraft "looked like a snake swallowing three mice.") There was no foreplane, but long chines ran from the wing to the nose, and two small vertical fins were canted inward. There were no ventral fins.

It all seemed needlessly complex from the aerodynamic and structural viewpoints. The wing-mounted engines created a problem in the engine-out case, called for long control and subsystem runs, and meant that an awkward structure was needed to carry the wing loads around the engine bay. The absence of a foreplane meant higher landing speeds or an oversized wing, while the chines and the small vertical fins created a layout that was distinctly unstable at high speeds. The omission of ventral fins from a high-Mach design was also strange, since fins working in the high-pressure zone beneath the body are a great help to directional stability.

Reduced RCS was one of the main reasons for the design's odd appearance. Two-dimensional wedge inlets, canards and ventral fins fell into the category of retro-reflectors and were ruled out. The wing-mounted engines and slim fuselage created a slender side profile, and the chines and blending meant that incoming radar waves struck the body at an oblique angle. Many of the features had a dual purpose: The chines provided lift and favorable trim at high speed, and the inward-canted fins reduced radar echoes and eliminated an unfavorable rolling effect encountered with upright fins.

There was more to the design than met the eye. Radar-absorbent plastic material was used on the wing leading edges and control surfaces. At least one A-12 had plastic-skinned chines, and all-plastic vertical fins were also tested. The plastic fins were not standardized, because they did not make much difference to the RCS.

The effect of all this work was largely academic. The performance of the A-12 and SR-71 was sufficient to defeat any defensive system, and the SR-71 traded some observability for payload by reverting to metal chines containing sensor bays. There is also some mixed evidence for the effectiveness of the low-RCS measures. When an SR-71 broke all transatlantic speed records on a flight to the Farnborough Air Show in Britain in September 1974, the British Plessey company, manufacturer of the civil surveillance radar covering the Atlantic approach, announced proudly that its AR-5D system had picked up the Blackbird over 200 miles away and accurately measured its (classified) cruising altitude. The USAF was less than amused by this revelation, which was made in all innocence. At the time, there had been no mention of the reduced-observables technology incorporated in the SR-71, and the term "Stealth" had never been used in public.

On the other hand, it has been reported that the SR-71 is sometimes seen on its approach to landing before it is detected by radar. One hypothesis to cover this apparent anomaly is that the tremendous heat of the airframe at Mach 3 causes ionization in the upper atmosphere, and it is this phenomenon that is picked up on radar. In that case, too, the low-observability features could be important, because they prevent a hostile system from discriminating between ionized air and the aircraft.

The A-12, however, came too late to save the United States' manned overflight program. On May 1, 1960, just under two years before the A-12 flew, a U-2 was shot down over Sverdlovsk in the USSR. The US government made matters worse by lying about its mission, before it was realized that the pilot had survived and was in Soviet custody. No later US administration took such a risk again, particularly as reconnaissance satellites, which were close to service status at that time, could acquire data safely and legally.

This 147T, seen under the wing of its DC-130A carrier, is a flight-test article; the screen over its inlet is a ground-safety device rather than a radar shield. Thirty-three surviving Model 147Ts, stored in the mid-seventies, were sold to Israel in 1984. (Teledyne Ryan Aeronautical)

continue the program. In 1964, the drones were tested operationally over mainland China. Eventually, a bewildering series of Model 147 subtypes was built and operated, and the Lightning Bugs, as they were called, were a major asset to photographic and electronic reconnaissance operations over Vietnam.

Early operational versions were not usually "treated" and many were shot down by SAMs, including four by Chinese SA-2s. Even so, they proved to be difficult targets for fighters, and brought back a great deal of high-resolution photographs from very high risk areas. Later versions of the series, such as the re-engined, long-span Model 147T, were equipped with an array of radar-absorbent components known as HIDE (high-absorbency integrated defense), to reduce reflection from the engine and airframe.

Despite the failure of the Red Wagon program to gain approval in 1960, the idea of a low-observables unmanned strategic reconnaissance system remained alive. By September 1961, seven major manufacturers had proposed such systems. The Pentagon was looking for an unmanned, high-resolution system that would be independent of bases outside the United States. The reasons for an unmanned system were partly technical (detectability would be greatly reduced and performance increased, if provisions for a pilot were eliminated) but mainly political. The US government had

Another advanced reconnaissance system was the D-21 drone. Sharing many features with the SR-71, the D-21 is thought to have made even more extensive use of radar-absorbent materials and other Stealth features. (Jay Miller/Aerofax)

promised not to send manned overflights across the Soviet Union, but a pilotless machine was another matter. Finally, two advanced reconnaissance systems were developed, starting in the early sixties. Only one of them was used operationally, and it was retired in 1972. Details of both programs remain obscure, and very little has been released officially.

Given the ban on manned overflights—the very operations for which the A-12 was designed—it was not surprising that Lockheed put forward a modification of the system to overcome political objections. This was a very high speed, expendable drone, powered by a ramjet engine and launched from the A-12. This aircraft, the D-21, was developed by the Lockheed Missiles & Space Company in collaboration with the Skunk Works, and is believed to have started flight tests in 1966.

In its planform and profile, the D-21 resembled an A-12 nacelle and outer wing. It was highly blended, with room for reconnaissance sensor bays on either side of the ramjet duct. Data was stored in an ejectable capsule, to be recovered by a mid-air snatch operation at the end of the reconnaissance run. The type made more extensive use of radar-transparent and radar-absorbent material than ever before, and the tail pipe was extended to mask the infrared signature. In conjunction with the vehicle's small size, this was expected to render it virtually undetectable.

The basic concept raises an interesting question: If the D-21 itself was designed for overflight, why was it to be launched from a high-speed, penetrating, reconnaissance aircraft? This suggests some interesting mission profiles, in which the A-12/D-21 combination would make a "fire alarm" incursion into unfriendly airspace. Having

Side view of a D-21 shows its slender profile, blending between the vertical fin and the body, and what appears to be a radar-absorbent blanket on its upper surface. The long tail pipe may have been designed to suppress the IR signature from the Marquardt RJ43 ramjet engine. (Jay Miller/Aerofax)

scrambled the defenses, the A-12 would launch the D-21 under heavy jamming cover, turn and escape; in the confusion, the tiny target represented by the D-21 might penetrate undetected. The range of the D-21 has not been revealed, apart from a statement that it was "in excess of thousands of miles."

The other drone was developed by Ryan under the Compass Arrow program, and bore a strong resemblance to the Model 136 proposal. Designated Model 154 by the company and AQM-91A by the USAF, it was ordered in 1966 and flew in 1969. Like the Model 136, it had a flat underside, a dorsal engine shielded by the fuselage and twin inward-canted fins. It was a large aircraft, powered by an 8,000-pound-thrust General Electric J97 engine—it was the only aircraft to use that engine, an ancestor of today's F404 turbofan—and had a span of forty-eight feet. Unusual features included electrically actuated flight controls.

This drone's intended mission was never discussed, but it was probably designed to take over from the extensively modified high-altitude Firebee drones, which were at greater risk from SAMs than the low-level versions. With its low-observables design and, presumably, the use of radar-absorbent structure, the AQM-91A would be more survivable than the modified Firebees. It was also capable of carrying larger and more powerful sensors, such as the sixty-six-inch focal length, long-range oblique photography (LOROP) cameras developed for the U-2. Like the earlier Lightning Bugs, Compass Arrow was essentially a "theater" system, launched and directed from a C-130 carrier aircraft and recovered by parachute.

Compass Arrow was still under development in 1972. The US withdrawal from Vietnam was well under way, and peace talks were progressing. In a related event in

Originally designed for launch from an SR-71, the D-21 was used operationally from a modified B-52D. The drone was used for clandestine, and apparently undetected, flights over China from around 1968 to 1972. (Lockheed)

that year, President Richard Nixon visited Beijing and agreed to halt overflights of mainland China. Both the D-21 and the AQM-91A were thereby robbed of their primary missions, and both programs were terminated in the period 1972-73. With the winding down of USAF operations in Vietnam, the drone operation became something of an orphan; after being transferred from Strategic Air Command (SAC) to Tactical Air Command (TAC), the entire drone program was halted in 1975.

The drones, however, had not been the only low-observables reconnaissance aircraft used in Vietnam. One of the main problems in that conflict was tracking an enemy who could move large forces and substantial amounts of equipment at night,

Another aircraft designed to complete its mission undetected—and, like the D-21, developed by Lockheed Missiles & Space Company—was the YO-3A quiet reconnaissance aircraft used by the US Army in Vietnam. Note the broad-chord three-blade propeller and prominent mufflers. Primary reconnaissance sensor is a side-looking airborne radar (SLAR) on the starboard side of the rear fuselage. (Lockheed Missiles & Space Company)

At this point, however, the history of the low-observables technology changes its nature. As the word "Stealth" began to be applied to all the ways of making aircraft less subject to detection, a pall of secrecy descended on the subject. An observer in the unclassified realm can do little more than piece together what fragmentary reports appear and try to sort out a coherent picture.

The technology also became more complex and more challenging, and straightforward optical analogies begin to lose their effectiveness. Before looking at what little we know about the Stealth aircraft of the seventies and eighties, it is important to look in detail at how targets are detected and how detection can be made more difficult.

Shown here is the Q-Star with an experimental six-blade wooden propeller. (Lockheed Missiles & Space Company)

CHAPTER 3

Design for Stealth

There is a classic and ancient cartoon that is probably found in every aircraft design office in the world. It shows an aircraft as each group in the team designed it. The aerodynamics group's design is smooth and flowing; the production group's contribution is usually represented by four planks, nailed together in the shape of an airplane; the maintenance group's design is a mass of access panels, with all the control runs on the outside; and so on. This cartoon would not be so widely circulated if it were not true to life. Every aircraft design embodies a compromise because many of the mission requirements tend to "push" the design in different ways.

There is one group, however, which is seldom identified on the cartoon—and, once again, this omission reflects reality. In most design offices, the electronic warfare (EW) group has very little influence on the design. Despite the importance of EW in many decisive air battles, EW specialists have had to fight for every watt of electrical power, every cubic foot of electronics bay and every square inch of surface area that they need to drive and accommodate processing equipment and antennae. The influence of EW on the basic configuration of most modern aircraft is precisely zero. But, if another sketch was to be added to the cartoon—"as the EW group saw it"—the result would be very close to a Stealth aircraft.

The EW group's world of radio frequencies, radar and jamming is where Stealth makes its first impact. It is not the only area of concern. Any vehicle, as it moves and functions, generates disturbances in the physical world around it, which propagate through space as waves. It puts out infrared radiation due to its warmth. Its noise and vibration send waves through the fluid air that surrounds it. It absorbs and reflects natural light in different proportions. All these disturbances are characteristics of the vehicle, and they make it possible for a distant observer to identify the vehicle. They are called "signatures" because they are both unique and a means of identification. Stealth calls for all these signatures to be controlled by the design of the aircraft; the particular importance of the radar signature is that it is by far the most prominent signature, and it is the one that provides an observer with the greatest amount of useful information at the greatest distance. Without controlling the radar signature, it is impossible to achieve Stealth.

Some understanding of the way in which radar waves affect a target (in radar jargon, anything observed by radar is a target) is a great help in comprehending the challenges and impact of Stealth. When we talk of a radar "seeing" a target, we think in terms of human sight. The analogy is accurate in some ways and misleading in others.

Eyes and telescopes work in the optical spectrum. The wavelength of visible light is much shorter than that of radar, which is why it is absorbed and distorted in the atmosphere, and its frequency is higher. The primary difference, though, is that we see in a world saturated with visible light energy. In order to see a target, a radar system first has to provide its own energy. It is rather like using a flashlight to find a small model aircraft in a pitch-black, lightless concert hall.

Any radar system searches a volume of space for targets by scanning it rapidly with a controlled beam of energy. When this plays across a target, the effect is the same as when the flashlight beam shines on the model aircraft: The target becomes visible, and the direction in which the flashlight is pointing gives the target's elevation and bearing. However, there are more lessons to be drawn from this analogy. The target is visible not only to the observer holding the flashlight, but also to the observer standing elsewhere in the hall; the energy from the flashlight is not reflected directly back to the observer, but is scattered in many different directions. Also, the characteristics of the target make it visible to a greater or lesser degree. If the model aircraft is white in color, it may be picked out easily. If it is highly polished, it will "glint"; the observer will see patches of light on its surface that seem almost as bright as the flashlight. If it is matt black in color, and its surroundings are nonreflective, it may be very difficult to see at all.

If the model moves, its image will change. If its wing is turned down toward the radar, it will probably be more visible than if it is viewed side-on. Obviously, its shape

The eye of the fighter aircraft is its powerful, long-range search radar, such as the GEC Avionics Foxhunter developed for the Royal Air Force's Tornado F.2 interceptor. Not only can a modern radar detect and track an aircraft, but it can also, in some cases, identify its type. (GEC Avionics)

defines just how much its image changes. The glint from a polished model will change constantly as the model moves.

Other targets may have completely different characteristics. A flat mirror might seem likely to be highly visible, but unless its surface makes two right angles to the beam (that is to say, it is "normal" to the beam), it reflects all the light away from an observer. A bowling ball does the opposite; it always reflects the same amount of light, regardless of its position.

Light energy striking an object usually goes one of three ways: It is reflected, absorbed or refracted. What is seen, except in the case of a clear bubble or a window, is mostly reflection modified by absorption of some frequencies. Because optical wavelengths are so short, most surfaces appear rough to a light wave, and energy is scattered randomly. Very smooth surfaces, however, will reflect a concentration of light at an angle opposite to the incident wave. This is the glinting phenomenon, technically known as specular reflection.

Radar energy acts in a somewhat different way, although the basic phenomena are the same. One very important point is that, because radar wavelengths are long, most synthetic surfaces are smooth to radar, and highly concentrated specular reflection is usually present. Just as a polished metal aircraft will glint blindingly in almost any direction on a bright summer day, so will its complex shape create radar glints in any direction. This very efficient reflection accounts for the extreme range at which radar can detect targets.

Radar waves are also scattered by other means. A radar beam is an electromagnetic field, and it generates a sympathetic field in any conductive object on which it impinges; as well as being a target, the object becomes an antenna. Irregularities in the

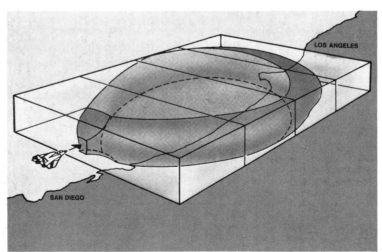

Fitted to the F-14 Tomcat (one of the world's best interceptors), the Hughes AWG-9 radar can pick up an average-sized target some 150 miles away. (Hughes)

One increasingly important tool for verifying the Stealth qualities of a design before the aircraft is built is the RCS range. One type of RCS range consists of a large chamber, lined on walls, floor and ceiling with plastic-foam pyramids. The function of the pyramids is to eliminate all echoes, and make the room electronically similar to free space. At one end of the room is a tower, carrying a model to be tested on top; at the other end are a radar transmitter and receiver. The radar system works in the high-frequency millimeter waveband, so that the wavelengths are scaled down in proportion to the model. The radar illuminates the model, and the high-resolution receiver analyzes the return. The RCS range commissioned by Vought Aerospace and Defense Division in 1984 is connected to a color monitor and plotter; it can display a synthetic television picture of the target, with the strength of the radar returns from each part of the airframe mapped in color, and immediately print a hard, full-color copy.

Advanced electronics make another contribution to Stealth. Since the early sixties, improvements in automatic flight control systems (AFCS) technology have steadily relaxed the formerly rigid requirement that any aircraft should be naturally stable about all three axes. In place of natural stability, the modern military aircraft is fitted with multiple systems of rate sensors and accelerometers which sense any deviations from the commanded flightpath and send electronic signals (as often as forty times every second) to the control actuators to correct the deviation before the pilot is even aware of it. The technology of these electronically signaled "fly-by-wire" systems has become steadily more reliable and more capable. The Lockheed A-12 was the first aircraft to depend on artificial stability in part of its flight envelope. Just over ten years later, in 1974, the F-16 was flown with artificial stability in the pitch axis. After ten more

Blending was incorporated on the SR-71 and B-1 partly to reduce RCS. Fortunately, its effects on overall airframe efficiency are beneficial. An early example, remarkably reminiscent of the B-1 from this angle, was the McDonnell XP-67 fighter. (McDonnell Douglas)

years, in 1984, the Grumman X-29 became the most grossly unstable aircraft ever to fly, and one of the first to rely totally on artificial stability in order to leave the ground. Similar technology frees the Stealth designer to follow the dictates of RCS as the shape of the aircraft is defined.

This design process starts by eliminating the efficient reflectors found on conventional designs. The biggest contributions to RCS, over the widest angle, come from retro-reflectors—plane surfaces at ninety degrees to one another. Such devices are built intentionally for use on target drones and small boats, where it is important to achieve a large RCS. Sometimes, too, they are inadvertently designed into aircraft, at the intersections of the wing and fuselage, where pylons attach to the wing or where the tailplane and fin meet. An incoming radar signal then bounces off the fin, strikes the tailplane and, if the angle between the two is ninety degrees, the main lobe is neatly turned around through a total of 180 degrees and fired straight back to the transmitter.

Retro-reflectors can be eliminated from the basic shape of the aircraft by canting the fins and the body sides, and, as far as possible, reducing the number of major components in the external shape. Many pre-Stealth fighters, for example, have extra fins beneath the tail; these provide a great deal of extra stability at high speed, but because of their relationship to the body they make a disproportionately large contribution to RCS.

Removing other retro-reflectors can be more difficult. The versatility of a modern fighter such as the F-16 springs from the fact that the tactical commander has a great

The conventional strike fighter carries its ordnance externally, in clusters on multiple ejection racks. The RCS contribution of such a layout is enormous, and alternatives have to be found for Stealth aircraft. (McDonnell Douglas)

deal of freedom to trade speed and maneuverability for fuel and weapons, by carrying extra weapons and high-capacity fuel tanks on underwing pylons. However, external stores and weapon pylons almost invariably introduce multiple reflections, and conventional external weapon carriage is incompatible with Stealth. The USAF's Advanced Tactical Fighter (ATF) may use some type of "conformal" weapon carriage, with its missiles recessed into ventral troughs, but aircraft such as the ATB and the Lockheed machine, which depend primarily on Stealth to survive and complete their missions, carry all their weapons internally. One problem for the designer of a Stealth aircraft is that external fuel tanks can no longer be used to meet long-range mission requirements; all the fuel must be carried internally, so the aircraft will tend to be bigger and heavier for a similar performance.

The next most important RCS villain is the vertical or near-vertical plane surface. Traditional designs contain many of these. Rectangular-section, slab-sided fuselages are popular, because they make for easy packing of avionics and other systems. Fighters have large vertical fins, mainly to ensure adequate stability with a heavy load of external bombs. Such surfaces can be eliminated from a design by several means. Blending the wing smoothly into the fuselage sides is the best-known method, and was practiced on the F-16 and the B-1. Vertical fins can be canted inward. The cant angle has to be fairly sharp, probably in excess of thirty degrees from the vertical, to divert side-lobe reflections away from an airborne radar which may be above the target.

Cavities such as engine inlets and the cockpit are great contributors to RCS. They are at least equivalent to flat plates of the same area—depending on what is in them, they may be worse—and they are visible over wider angles at more sensitive aspects. The inlets, for example, tend to be most visible in frontal aspect, and give one of the first warnings of an aircraft's approach. This is because good inlet design is virtually equivalent to poor Stealth design. An efficient inlet is straight, any moving parts at its forward end are flat (for the sake of simplicity), and the distance from the inlet lip to the engine is as short as possible, to save weight. It can therefore act as a conduit for radar waves to reach the compressor face of the engine. Not only does this represent a large mass of solid metal, but its shape and movement put a characteristic beat in the radar return. Very advanced fighter radars, such as the Hughes APG-70 and APG-71 (fitted to the latest F-15 Eagles and to the new F-14D Tomcat, respectively), include digital electronic processors which are so fast that they can actually count the compressor blades and positively identify the aircraft type at a distance of almost 100 miles.

In the case of a dedicated very low level or very high level aircraft, it should be possible to shield the inlets above or below the body. The problem is more involved when the defending radar may be either above or below the intruder. Regardless of position, the inlet is likely to have a long duct, a change in section and special internal features. The inlet system changes made in the development of the B-1B from the original B-1 show some steps in the right direction: The variable ramps were eliminated, the inlet lips and splitter were swept back from the vertical, and curved longitudinal baffles were installed in the duct, so that the front face of the engine could not be seen from the outside. The inlets included a radar-absorbent liner, of the type discussed in more detail below.

Long, curved, baffled ducts can considerably reduce the contribution of the engines to RCS. Dedicated Stealth aircraft may also feature flush inlets; a workable configuration was developed in the forties and used on a number of early jet aircraft, and has recently been used as an auxiliary inlet on aircraft and racing cars. The largest such inlets were those used on the North American YF-93 fighter, feeding a 5,000-pound-thrust engine, so there are probably no insuperable problems involved in adapting flush inlets to modern aircraft. The main advantage of the flush inlet is that the inlet aperture is visible to radar over a smaller range of angles than is the case with a conventional design. The problem, as with all techniques for concealing the engines from view, is to keep the inevitable penalties in weight and airflow restriction within reasonable limits.

Blocking the inlet with wire mesh, as long as the mesh spacing is no more than a fraction of the radar wavelength, reduces RCS quite effectively. However, the main threat to the reconnaissance drones on which this was first tried was long-wavelength surface-to-air missile and surveillance radar; protection against centimeter-wavelength fighter radars would require a tighter mesh, possibly aerodynamically unacceptable.

Semiconformal weapon carriage, as used for the four belly-mounted Sparrow missiles on this F-4, is a proven way of reducing drag and RCS. However, it may not be enough for a dedicated Stealth aircraft, which may have to carry all its weapons in internal bays. (McDonnell Douglas)

Supersonic low-observables inlets are a special problem because flush inlets are probably unacceptable at the high speeds at which these aircraft fly. Vertical ramp-type inlets are excellent retro-reflectors and have a very large RCS. Some impressions of high-speed Stealth types have shown half-cone inlets; such inlets can be blended into the underside of the aircraft, they have a narrow aperture and they can be effectively treated with absorbent materials, but the shape of the inlets is such that the airflow does not have to negotiate any drastic changes in the duct section before reaching the face of the compressor.

Similar considerations apply to the exhaust cavities; again, propulsive efficiency and weight considerations favor a short, straight tube which leaves the rear face of the engine fully exposed over a wide arc. Some sources refer to a venetian blind exhaust, implying the use of slats narrow enough to suppress radar reflections from the rear of the engine. High-aspect-ratio nozzles, resembling narrow slots in the trailing edge, limit their high RCS contribution to a narrower range of angles. The exhaust can also be shielded by vertical fins.

The most effective way of reducing the RCS from the cockpit cavity is to eliminate both the canopy and the pilot; if a covert mission can be performed by a remotely-piloted or autonomous vehicle, so much the better. In the case of a manned aircraft, the cockpit cavity calls for detailed treatment, inside and out. The profile of the cavity should be kept down, and for a large aircraft such as the ATB, which is unlikely to engage in visual combat, a flush cockpit may be acceptable. The canopy itself is likely to be coated with a thin film of metal (techniques for applying a layer of indium-tin oxide to a transparent surface, so that ninety-eight percent of the light still passes through,

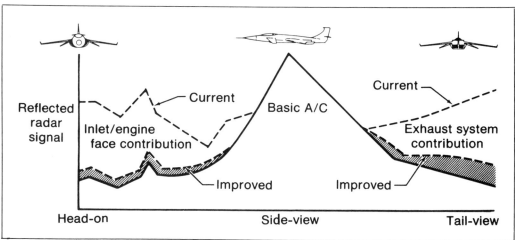

This chart shows how the inlet, engine face and exhaust account for the greatest part of the total radar reflection from an aircraft (top line) when it is nose-on or tail-on to the radar. On a future combat aircraft, the inlet and exhaust contribution will be reduced (shaded zone) so that it is only a small fraction of the total. (Pratt & Whitney)

have been developed) so that radar waves from outside are kept out of the cockpit, while radio-frequency emissions from inside, such as those from cathode-ray tube (CRT) displays and computers, are prevented from getting out.

Another form of cavity is the gap between the airframe and a control surface. Stealth aircraft may feature all-moving vertical and horizontal tail surfaces, carefully faired at the root to avoid gaps. Ailerons may be covered with flexible skins, as on the variable-camber flaps of the USAF's F-111 Mission Adaptive Wing research aircraft.

Some of these features—the need to carry weapons internally, to bury the engines inside long inlet and exhaust ducts, and to avoid steep vertical slopes—inevitably push the Stealth aircraft toward a highly blended configuration. If blending is taken to extremes, the result is either a flying wing or a lifting body. These two apparently opposite concepts are basically the same thing, differing mainly in their aspect ratios. The Northrop ATB is a flying wing; the Lockheed Stealth fighter is generally believed to make some use of body lift, and any forthcoming Stealth replacement for the SR-71 is likely to resemble a lifting-body configuration.

Detail shaping for Stealth is one of the most difficult and sensitive aspects of the technology. Some observations are fairly clear: Large flat surfaces and acute angles are to be avoided. It seems, however, that the attainment of the levels of RCS needed by new aircraft calls for some unusual and, at first sight, bizarre design features.

Published impressions of Stealthy aircraft have suggested that the avoidance of straight lines is a key to the RCS, but this is only part of the story. While a plane surface generates a strong glint at one angle, a simple curve generates a glint over a much wider range of angles. When a surface is large and slightly curved, this glint may be very

The NACA-type flush inlet was used for the North American YF-93 fighter, and could be improved for use on future Stealth designs. (Rockwell)

strong. One way of avoiding this problem is to avoid long, constant curves, using compound (three-dimensional) curvature and changing the curve radius constantly. This is another Stealth technique which has become a great deal easier with the advent of computer-aided design. (Curvature may not be the only answer, as we will see when we look at the Lockheed Stealth fighter.)

Would an aircraft laid out according to these principles be truly Stealthy? Probably not. A low-RCS configuration is the basis for Stealth, and it is impossible to achieve low RCS if the shape is fundamentally wrong. But the effect of eliminating the gross contributors to RCS, very often, is to leave a very substantial RCS generated by many smaller features of the aircraft. Also, while a good basic configuration may eliminate the worst glints, or direct them into areas where radar detection is improbable, the RCS levels needed by a Stealth aircraft imply that the side lobes, too, are to be controlled and aimed away from the hostile transmitter.

Again, these are due to the particular characteristics of the radar wave and the electromagnetic field it generates around the aircraft. Sharp edges and small-radius curves, small cavities, physical breaks in the skin (such as access panels and structural joints) and changes in the skin material (such as a transition from a metal fuselage panel to a graphite-epoxy access door) all generate eddies and disturbances in the field. Cannon muzzles can be a particular problem. At very low levels of RCS, even a row of steel fastener heads in an aluminum skin can be significant. The target aircraft's own communications, navigation and IFF (identification friend-or-foe) antennae make naturally good passive reflectors. A forward-looking radar antenna is the worst of all; to a hostile radar, it looks like a cat's eye in a headlight beam.

Some of these echoes can be eliminated through detail design: eliminating unnecessary skin breaks, carefully matching materials, covering gun muzzles with sliding panels and so on. However, at this level of RCS, special materials play an important part. Almost every person in the United States, and an increasing proportion of people in the rest of the world's richer nations, routinely exploits the fact that different materials respond to high-frequency electromagnetic waves in different ways. The common microwave oven, invented by radar engineers just after World War II, is no more than a simple, powerful radar transmitter. Its design and operation illustrate a few basic points about radar and materials.

The oven's antenna and cooking area are surrounded by a light steel shield. Because steel is electrically conductive, the shield is an efficient reflector, and prevents radiation from reaching the outside. The door is glass, but is provided with a wire-mesh screen. The mesh spacing is much smaller than a wavelength, so it also reflects the radar waves. (As noted above, a similar technique can be used on aircraft inlets.) Any conductive material put in the oven (a common mistake is to use a plate with a gold ring) will reflect the waves, possibly in the alarming form of arcing.

One of the most convenient features of a microwave oven is that glass and ceramic containers do not get hot; radar waves pass through them. The same goes for some thermoplastics. Structural materials based on these substances, such as fiberglass, have similar characteristics. Because of their basic molecular structure, these materials are almost completely nonconductive, or dielectric (ceramics and plastics are widely used for insulators and electrical components) and are virtually transparent to radar, irrespective of wavelength. This is why such materials, ceramics and fiberglass in particular, are used for radomes. They have recently been joined by artificial materials, such as Kevlar, a dielectric aramid fiber which is used in much the same way as fiberglass but has a higher tensile strength.

Some dielectrics, such as fiberglass and Kevlar, can be used for primary aircraft structure, but will not automatically mean a low RCS. The reverse is often true. The dielectric structure may simply allow the radar waves to pass through and be reflected by all the internal metal components, including the engine. On a radar screen, one designer has said, the result "looks like a big cloud of chaff." However, if dielectrics form part of a properly designed structure, another factor may come into play. Just as glass and water "bend" light, radar-transparent materials refract radar waves. A glass or Kevlar honeycomb, properly designed, can distort incoming waves and reduce the size of the main lobe.

A microwave oven works because some materials are not reflective or transparent, but absorb microwave energy. The molecular structure of these materials is such that the radar waves cause the molecules to vibrate, and the radar energy is turned to heat. This principle applies to water (including that found in food, which is how the oven cooks), but it also applies to a variety of other materials, both dielectric and conductive, some of which form the basis for different kinds of radar-absorbent material or RAM.

Clearly visible in the foreground of this photograph, showing an A-12 structural-test specimen, is the saw-tooth pattern of RAM inserts in the leading edge of the wing. The lighter areas are titanium, and provide structural strength; the dark areas are RAM wedges. (Lockheed)

RAM has been in existence almost as long as radar itself. It has been used on ship structures, adjacent to the ships' own radars, so that the structure does not interfere with the radars. It is used in anechoic chambers, rooms in which the walls are lined with RAM to absorb all radar echoes. Such electronically dead rooms are used for testing and developing radar systems. The first defensive use of RAM was in the period 1944-45, when the conning towers of some German submarines were covered with absorbent material to reduce the risk of detection by radar-carrying Allied patrol aircraft. These early types of RAM were of no use to the aircraft designer, being heavy, bulky and structurally weak. No aircraft with enough RAM to make a significant difference to its RCS could ever perform a useful mission, even if it could fly and the RAM itself could stay together under air loads. Since then, companies have developed RAM for many purposes; and details of some of them have been published.

Perfect RAM (the Stealth designer's version of "unobtainium," the structural engineer's standard joke material) would be applied in the same way as paint, would absorb all wavelengths and would work equally well on radar waves impinging at any angle. Real RAM is different. All such materials absorb some wavelengths better than others. They absorb waves gradually, as they pass through the material, so the degree of absorption (usually measured in decibels) is proportional to the bulk and weight of RAM. Thus, lightweight RAM may be effective only over a narrow waveband, or at one angle.

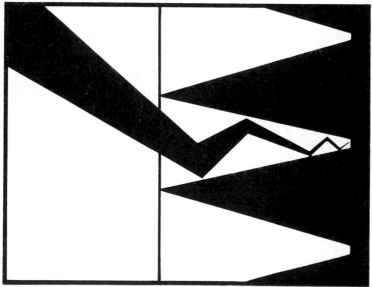

The principle of the A-12's absorbent structure is shown here. The acute wedge shape traps any incident radar beam, causing it to reflect from one side of the wedge to the other. As it does so, its energy is gradually absorbed into the RAM. (Hughes)

Only when aircraft designers began to look seriously at reduced RCS, and once they managed to achieve RCS reductions through configuration, did they enter the region where RAM could be a practical proposition. The first aircraft to make extensive use of RAM was the Lockheed A-12. Two types of RAM were used. One was a plastic honeycomb material developed by Lockheed's chemists, which was used on the wing leading and trailing edges of the A-12 and SR-71, and on the entire chine of the A-12. Remarkably, it could withstand high air loads, and 600°F temperatures. It was not strong enough to take the full loads on the A-12 leading edge, so it was incorporated in a specially designed structure. The load-carrying titanium ribs and skins formed a saw-toothed structure, which was filled in with V-shaped plastic inserts (this pattern can be seen clearly in many photographs).

The effect of this structure, which may be emulated by radar-absorbing structures on current Stealth aircraft, is interesting. Essentially, the principle is similar to the design of an anechoic chamber, with its ranks of pyramidical absorbers lining the walls. The absorbent material is not 100 percent effective. It reflects some radiation, and gradually absorbs the rest as it passes through. However, the acutely angled V shape forms a trap for the radar wave. In the case of the A-12 structure, only part of the radar energy is absorbed by the RAM, and the rest bounces off the titanium substructure. However, the geometry is such that the main lobe then bounces off the opposite side of the V, and continues to do so, losing energy with each bounce.

The other type of RAM developed for the A-12 was a paint known as ''iron ball,'' containing microscopic particles of an iron compound in the ferrite family. Such paints

This unusual view of an unpainted B-1B displays numerous black areas which may well indicate the presence of RAM: on the fin/tail-plane junction, around the root of the small ride-control canards, around the engine exhausts and nacelle/fuselage fillet, and on the leading and trailing edges of the tailplane. (Rockwell)

are not radar-proof; however, they do weaken the electromagnetic currents on the skin, helping to suppress some of the side lobes in a radar return. The same paint is used on U-2s.

Since the early sixties, considerably better types of RAM have been developed, some of which can be substituted for secondary structure (access panels and fairings, for example) for a minimal weight penalty. Others provide a great deal of absorbing power for moderate weight and bulk, and can be used to treat potential hot spots such as inlet ducts and necessary structural breaks. The RCS effect of antennae can be minimized by placing them in RAM-lined cavities.

RAM comes in many varieties, and the nature of the latest and most effective types is a closely guarded secret. Generally, however, RAM is made up of a number of different materials, assembled to provide the right blend of structural and electromagnetic properties. The "active ingredients" include carbon, an absorbent dielectric, and the magnetic iron compounds known as ferrites, which absorb energy as they conduct it. Some other materials have similar characteristics, such as the plastic invented by Lockheed and the hard-wearing cyanamide-based plastic usually known as melamine, which is used for unbreakable tableware. (Anyone who has unwittingly tried to use a melamine utensil in a microwave oven will know, from painful experience, how effective an absorber it is.)

Most of these absorbers, however, have poor structural characteristics, and no practicable aircraft can carry a sufficient thickness of solid absorber to make a significant difference to its RCS. Some kinds of practical RAM consist of carbon-impregnated foam core, with a radar-transparent Kevlar skin. Others take the form of a honeycomb material. Another type of RAM is a thin sandwich of several layers, each effective against a different frequency. RAM may be, literally, designed to absorb incoming energy, or it may be designed to distort it. Some RAM is designed to take structural loads, while some is not. Generally, the considerable advances in the development of strong nonmetallic structures, and in the art of bonding have made important contributions to the development of RAM, by making it possible to eliminate metal components from aircraft surfaces.

Carbon-fiber material, sometimes simply known as graphite, certainly plays a part in Stealth technology. (It was invented in Britain in the sixties, and was being studied for military airframes about the time that development of the Stealth concept began.) It is the only nonconducting, nonmetallic material which has so far been proved suitable for use in the primary structure of large, high-performance military aircraft. Like fiberglass and Kevlar (which are too flexible for highly loaded structures) carbon-fiber is used as a composite material; the high-strength fibers are held in a matrix material, usually an epoxy resin, which holds the fibers in place and gives the material stiffness and stability.

Carbon-fiber's electromagnetic characteristics fall between those of RAM and radar-transparent material. A structure with a carbon-fiber skin and metal spars and fasteners may have a high RCS because of echoes from the many flat surfaces and retro-reflectors in the substructure. On the other hand, carbon-fiber absorbs and reflects enough radiation to be unsuitable for use in radomes.

The Learfan 2100 business aircraft, almost entirely made of carbon fiber, is an example of how Stealth can be achieved unintentionally. As well as the composite airframe, it features a nonmetallic Kevlar propeller; a fuselage that incorporates constant compound curves, with very few breaks and no mechanical fasteners; engines that are completely buried in the fuselage; and a Y-shaped tail that has no retro-reflectors. The wing is unswept—this creates a large RCS in the nose-on aspect, but the RCS decreases rapidly with increasing angle off the nose. The Learfan's RCS is undoubtedly high by Stealth standards, but is low enough to cause problems for commercial surveillance radar systems. Accordingly, the Learfan is one of few business aircraft to carry two transponders, so that it can be picked up if one fails. (Unfortunately, development of this innovative airplane stopped in mid-1985 because of financial problems.)

A member of the carbon fiber family is reinforced carbon-carbon (RCC). Originally developed for missile nose cones, RCC is formed from carbon fibers in a special

The design of the Learfan executive aircraft gave rise to some concern that it might not be readily detected by civil surveillance radars. A nonmetallic airframe and propeller, completely buried engines (the fairings on the fuselage side are cowlings over the intakes and exhausts) and the absence of a large vertical fin reduced the type's RCS. (LearAvia)

matrix which is baked at a very high temperature until it carbonizes. RCC is radar-absorbent, structurally strong and relatively impervious to heat. A likely use is in engine tail pipes and exhaust nozzle components.

The latest carbon-fiber-based material to attract attention uses a thermoplastic matrix; it may be cheaper and easier to build and repair than the carbon-fiber/epoxy material in current use, and its electromagnetic qualities are, if anything, more attractive to the designer of a Stealth aircraft.

A Stealth aircraft is likely to use several different types of RAM: deep-sectioned RAM on leading and trailing edges; bulky, high-performance, broad-band RAM in the inlet ducts; structural RAM built into the skins; RCC in the jetpipes; and absorbent paint overall, to clear up surviving side lobes. However, different types of RAM have to be used with care, to ensure that the boundaries between materials of different conductivity do not cause their own hot spots in the aircraft's radar image.

Finally, new materials are being developed which are not exactly RAM, but which contribute to the control of the aircraft's radar signature. Among them are special lightweight foils and scrims (very light, expanded metal sheets) which are used to create precisely tailored patterns of conductivity and, possibly, to form one-way filters that will let radar waves pass in, but will tend to trap the weakened echo. There are also tapelike materials, apparently used to bridge structural gaps.

Looking at the number of variables—configuration, aspect, wavelength, structural material and RAM—which affect the observability of the aircraft, it is easy to see why the design of a Stealth aircraft was not attempted until computer modeling had become a feasible technique. Verifying the levels of RCS achieved by such methods calls for new testing techniques. Millimeter-wave RCS ranges give good scale results, but full-scale ranges are used for the final verification of RCS at real-world wavelengths. (The USAF has one, at Wright-Patterson AFB, and so do major Stealth contractors such as Lockheed and Northrop.) Construction of a full-scale mockup of a new design, specifically for RCS tests, may be required under the ATF program, and emphasizes an important aspect of the technology: RCS control is still not an exact science.

Drastic reductions in RCS are, therefore, possible, even though they represent a monstrous design challenge and call for rethinking virtually every design priority in the book. But Stealth technology is like a game of Dungeons & Dragons, in which success at one level qualifies the player to tackle a new set of ogre-infested mazes. Once the RCS has been pulled down where it belongs, the aircraft's other signatures become dominant.

Thermal, or infrared (IR), signatures are second in importance to RCS. Apart from radar, the IR spectrum is the only one in which targets can be reliably detected beyond visual range; it is also the spectrum outside the radar bands in which air-to-air weapons, or autonomous anti-aircraft weapons of any kind, have been made to work. There are at least three aspects of the thermal signature: the heat of the engine components, the heat of the exhaust and other emissions from the aircraft, and the heat of the aircraft itself. All objects, except those at absolute zero, radiate a pattern of heat, and thus have a thermal image.

The hot metal of an engine is the strongest source of IR radiation. It will probably be necessary to provide the Stealth aircraft with an exhaust system which obscures the hottest parts of the engine from as many angles as possible. A useful technology here may be the two-dimensional (2-D) nozzle, already under development for the Advanced Tactical Fighter. On dry thrust, in the closed position, the 2-D nozzle restricts the rear view of the engines to a very narrow angle. Were it to be fabricated in RCC, it would suppress both radar and thermal signatures.

The exhaust plume and the point where it leaves the aircraft are also a potential problem. There is a necessary compromise here: High-bypass turbofan engines, like airliner engines, have the coolest exhaust flows, but their large mass flows and diameters would make it very difficult to install them behind effective low-RCS inlets. For this reason, Stealth aircraft will probably use medium-bypass-ratio turbofan engines, with integral hot/cold flow mixers. The 2-D exhaust system has potential here, because

Electro-optical detection systems are becoming increasingly important as a back-up to radar, and present a new problem for a Stealth aircraft. This long-focus stabilized television camera is used to identify targets for the F-14 at long range. The new F-14D will couple this system with an infrared tracker. (Northrop)

efficient variable geometry can be incorporated with relative ease. It might, for example, be designed with a set of forward flaps that would allow cold outside air to be drawn in and mixed with the engine exhaust. This would reduce the peak thermal signature at a cost in efficiency, but it would only need to be done in a high-threat area.

The thermal signatures from the airframe are becoming more important as thermal-sensing and image-processing technologies improve. Fighter aircraft have been carrying infrared search and track systems (IRSTS) since the early sixties, and most Soviet fighters use IRSTS as a back-up in case the radar is jammed. The USAF and US Navy are working on a new IRSTS which will be more reliable and less prone to false alarms than earlier systems. Its range is secret, but in clear air at high altitude, against a bomber-size target, it may not be far short of 100 miles. In the tactical regime, SAM systems based solely on the thermal detection and tracking of targets are not far off.

While it is impossible to eliminate IR radiation, it might be possible to reduce the enemy's chance of detecting it. The reason is that only two bands of IR radiation propagate at all well through the atmosphere, while others are absorbed. With a combination of some kind of airframe cooling, using the fuel as a heat sink as the SR-71 does, and special coatings, it might be possible to tailor the thermal signature so that most of the heat is emitted at wavelengths which the atmosphere would absorb. In addition, a Stealth aircraft will use closed-loop systems to cool the cabin air and avionics, all designed to minimize the amount of heat dumped overboard.

Acoustic and optical signatures are also significant issues. The former, however, tend to be solved as a by-product of controlling RCS and the thermal signature. The clean configuration; long, baffled engine inlet; medium-bypass engine; and mixed exhaust of a Stealth aircraft will make it extremely quiet in operation. It is hard to see what more could be done to reduce noise.

Avoiding detection by the naked eye or tracking by electro-optical systems may be more difficult. Operating at night is one approach, but is impractical for the ATB, which uses Polar routes for crucial phases of its missions—daylight may last twenty-four hours in summer. Another is to reduce the side-on and head-on profiles of the aircraft; films of the YB-49 flying wing bomber show how the aircraft virtually disappears from view as it turns head-on to the camera, although the dense trails of black smoke from the eight J35s gave it away.

One intriguing concept that has been discussed is active camouflage. This would involve installing an illumination system aboard the aircraft, controlled by photo-electric sensors, which would automatically illuminate each surface of the aircraft to match its background. It might not fool a human observer, but it might deceive the cruder processing equipment of an electro-optical system.

It is true to say that RCS reduction is the most important issue in Stealth. However, the radar return from an aircraft is not always its most powerful signature, nor the one by which it is most easily identified. That dubious honor, all too often, belongs to its own sensors and avionics systems. There is a simple reason for this. A radar signal is transmitted by an antenna over a definite arc, and becomes less dense as it goes out. A small portion of the signal is intercepted by a target and scattered over a wide area. A tiny portion of this signal is received back by the radar.

An active electronic emission from a target, on the other hand, is scattered only once, when it leaves the target. It also has to go only half as far before it is received. The classic example of this was the Monica tail-warning radar, used for a brief but disastrous period by the Bomber Command of the Royal Air Force in 1943-44. At a time when the range of a fighter radar was tens of miles under the best possible conditions, the Flensburg passive homing device was developed by the Luftwaffe, after finding Monica sets on shot-down bombers. It could pick up targets over England from an aircraft over Germany.

The challenge is to prevent such emissions from being detected while making it possible for a Stealth aircraft to find its targets and go about its mission. The best way to do this would be to eliminate emissions completely, through the use of passive, nonemitting devices.

Some solutions to the problem are in hand. For a Stealth fighter, a forward-looking infrared (FLIR) system can be used for low-level navigation or attack at night, as long as its inability to operate in clouds or rain is acceptable. If an active (emitting) sensor is required, there may not be any need to put it on a strike aircraft; a Stealth fighter is likely to work in close coordination with its high-flying stablemate, the TR-1. Operating at 75,000 feet, to the rear of the battle, the TR-1 can detect and locate targets by active or passive means and direct a fighter, or a Stealth cruise missile, by datalink to the target area.

Under the nose of this Soviet Mikoyan MiG-23 Flogger-B fighter is a glass-fronted housing for an infrared search and track (IRST) system. These are standard on all Soviet fighters, and emphasize the importance of thermal signature control to a Stealth aircraft. (Tass)

Designers are now looking at advanced techniques for terrain-following/terrain-avoidance (TF/TA), or automated low-level navigation in three dimensions. As a result of the cruise-missile program, most of the world's potential combat zones have been computer-mapped, and techniques are being developed to use this data for combat-aircraft navigation. The USAF is testing a system which uses digital map data to plan the best-protected low-level track to any point selected by a pilot. Because the system knows, from stored data, what terrain lies ahead, it should need to rely very little on a forward-looking radar. The British Aerospace TERPROM (terrain profile matching) system uses a similar database to provide a pilot with an indication of the terrain ahead, using a low-powered radar altimeter rather than a terrain-following radar.

The Stealth designer also must take into account the electronic noise generated by the airborne systems; this problem is analogous to that of ensuring the security of computer data. Such noise can be suppressed in several ways. Minimizing power and eliminating nonessential traffic are basic philosophical approaches and may reduce the problem at its source. Internal traffic can be reduced in volume and distance by grouping systems together, and fiber-optic cables, which cause no detectable emissions, can be used for longer runs. For example, there is no reason, apart from convenience, for the digital electronic engine controls (DEECs) to be attached physically to each engine; they receive and transmit data electronically. All four DEECs could be housed in a common bay, together with the flight control system, with which they would converse. Optical links would connect the bay with the engine and control surface actuators. One advantage is that suppressing electronic emissions leaving the aircraft, and protecting the systems against the electromagnetic pulse caused by nuclear explosions, both call for very similar measures.

This outline of some of the technologies that may be used on a Stealth aircraft leaves one vital observation to be made: The success of a Stealth aircraft depends not only on the individual component technologies, but on the skill with which they are blended to be effective against a wide range of known, projected and conceivable threats, without excessively penalizing the vehicle's combat capability.

One could hazard a guess that this art is the most sensitive part of Stealth, and the most compelling reason for the high security which has been imposed, and continues to be imposed, on the two biggest Stealth-dependent programs: the Northrop Advanced Technology Bomber and the first operational Stealth aircraft, the enigmatic, all-black Stealth strike fighter developed by the Lockheed Skunk Works.

CHAPTER 4

Stealth fighter

Few people would have argued that Lockheed, in the early seventies, was not a company of immense technical capability. Fewer still would have disputed the fact that it was in serious trouble, financially and commercially. The TriStar airliner, into which the company had plowed its Vietnam-era earnings, was behind schedule and over cost, because Rolls-Royce, the builder of its engines, had gone bankrupt. Lockheed had agreed to build the C-5 freighter at a fixed price, had experienced cost overruns and was trying to renegotiate the contract at a reduced but still staggering loss. The AH-56 strike helicopter was at the point of being canceled. The company was going to have to seek a US government loan guaranty in order to stay in business.

Even the Skunk Works was in trouble. The ADP operation was being scrutinized by new corporate managers, who wondered what it could contribute to the company. The banning of all reconnaissance flights over China, and the steady improvement of legal reconnaissance satellites, spelled an end of the market for clandestine spy planes. ADP had not delivered a new aircraft since the late sixties, and did not have any products that the USAF wanted; Lockheed-California had not won a USAF contract since the mid-sixties. After the company failed to win USAF support for a new fighter based on F-104 components in mid-1971, ADP was on the verge of closure.

It must have been around this time that the idea of a Stealth fighter—an ultra-low-detectability tactical strike and reconnaissance aircraft, based on techniques and technology developed for the A-12 and D-21—began to attract attention within ADP. It was something that nobody else was working on, and which nobody else could develop: in short, a typical ADP program.

The Linebacker raids, with the enormous effort devoted to electronic support, further stimulated thinking about Stealth. Even though the USAF remained outwardly convinced that chaff, jamming and suppression could carry the day, the sheer number of SAMs fired by the North Vietnamese managed, now and again, to overwhelm the EW effort. It was also known that the Soviet Union was placing a great deal of emphasis on the SAM, developing more new systems than the US and deploying them in larger numbers. Most of the new weapons were mounted on tracked vehicles, so the SAM belts would be harder to map than they had been in Vietnam.

During 1972 and 1973, ADP designers worked on the problems of Stealth aircraft: shape, performance, systems and weapons. It is probably safe to say that preliminary findings showed enough promise to keep ADP going, and to attract USAF interest.

The USAF itself had a low-budget program in this area. It had grown out of work by Dr. Leo Windecker, a Midland, Texas, designer who had worked throughout the sixties on the development of a high-efficiency, all-composite light plane called the Eagle. While the Eagle was made of radar-transparent materials and had a high RCS due to its internal metal components, Windecker saw the potential for a nonmetallic low-RCS aircraft, and had proposed such a development of Pentagon and White House officials as early as 1963. Nothing came to the proposal, but in 1972, after the prototype Eagle had been flying for some years, Windecker approached the USAF again with better results. The prototype Eagle was loaned to the USAF for RCS testing, and Windecker Aircraft received a contract for a specially designed, low-RCS prototype. This aircraft, designated YE-5A, was built in the same tooling as the Eagle, and was similar in appearance; internally, however, it used various absorbers and other techniques to reduce its RCS. The YE-5A was delivered to the USAF in 1973, and was tested by the USAF, Lockheed and later the US Army in various classified programs.

In October 1973, war broke out in the Middle East. Those who expected a rerun of June 1967, when the Israeli air force swarmed over its adversaries and decided the war in minutes, were in for a shock. The Egyptian armed forces had been equipped with the

The Windecker YE-5A was built for the US Air Force in 1973 to demonstrate the Stealth potential of nonmetallic airframes. Outwardly similar to the Windecker Eagle lightplane, the YE-5A had a dielectric fiberglass skin and internal RAM. It was used for a series of classified tests. (Dr. L. J. Windecker)

new Soviet SA-6 surface-to-air missile, using a completely different guidance system from the older SA-2 and SA-3. The Soviet Union had managed to keep the system secure, and no jamming system in Israeli service could cope with it. Better jammers were rushed to the scene by the United States and, together with improved tactics,

This impression of a Stealth strike aircraft appeared in a US National Research Council report, which was prepared by a team of senior US aerospace engineers. It is a two-seat, all-weather 50,000-pound subsonic aircraft powered by two modified nonafterburning General Electric F404s, without afterburning—the same powerplant is reported to be used on the Lockheed Stealth fighter—fitted with infrared-suppressing two-dimensional nozzles. Its most striking feature is the absence of vertical and horizontal stabilizers. Instead, it uses a combination of multipurpose wing surfaces and thrust vectoring. Note also the capacious ventral weapons bay; the aircraft could carry a 12,000 pound payload. The team expected that a design such as this could be fielded by 1995 or, with further improved technology, in the year 2000—the same time frame as the US Navy's proposed Advanced Tactical Aircraft. (National Research Council)

these turned the tide against the SA-6. But the losses suffered in the first few hours of combat by one of the world's most capable air forces had been a shock.

It may have been coincidence that the Lockheed Stealth strike fighter was funded in the following year, but it is unlikely. The lesson of October 1973, in terms of EW, was simple: There is always a risk of surprise in the war of jammers and radars, and surprise is very costly. One advantage of Stealth is that it is relatively little affected by changes in frequency and waveform, and is thus immune to the potential surprises inherent in EW techniques.

Lockheed's Stealth demonstration program is believed to have been funded by DARPA, under the code name Have Blue. The aircraft was also known as the XST (experimental, Stealth, tactical). According to one report, it was sometimes called Project Harvey, after the invisible six-foot rabbit that haunted James Stewart in the movie of the same name. A number of prototypes were built at Burbank between 1975 and 1977, and were ferried by truck or C-5 into Nevada.

Taken from the same report as the subsonic strike fighter design, this impression shows a supersonic short-take-off/vertical-landing (Stovl) fighter. Extensive blending, inward-canted fins and conformal inlet and exhaust systems are used to reduce RCS. (National Research Council)

Its destination was a flight-test facility within the vast weapons and practice range surrounding Nellis AFB. This site, first used to test the U-2 in the mid-fifties, was chosen because of the unparalleled security it offered. Like Edwards AFB, it was built on the edge of a dry lake, which provided a foundation for concrete runways and a large flat area for emergency landings; the airfield itself is usually called Groom Lake.

The site is not visible from outside the Nellis range, which is closed to the public and ringed by signs warning any would-be trespasser that unexploded ordnance is lying around and that the US government takes no responsibility for any unauthorized intruder who puts a foot or a wheel in the wrong place. Nellis is also an intensive airborne training area, under constant radar surveillance down to ground level, so the ban on civilian air traffic can be rigorously enforced. Most of the Lockheed people who work there do so under a further cover. They travel to Burbank each morning, and ride a company shuttle flight to Groom Lake. The facility started operations as a clutch of prefabricated buildings on the corner of the lake, but in the course of the A-12/SR-71 development program it expanded considerably, with a long paved runway and extensive data-processing equipment.

The first XST flew in early 1977. Most reports on the appearance of the Lockheed designs have been fairly consistent, indicating that the basic configuration has not changed to any great degree since that first aircraft. The Stealth fighter is about the same size as an F-4 or F-18, measuring about sixty feet from nose to tail. In planform, the

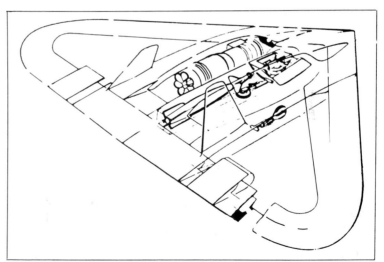

This study for a Tactical High-Altitude Penetrator (THAP) aircraft was prepared by a branch of the USAF's Aeronautical Systems Division, and was released in 1980. It is a flying wing with two buried turbofan engines and a deep layer of RAM—comprising nonconducting skins and foam cores—extending around its entire perimeter. The canted vertical fins, called rudderatorons, provide pitch, roll and yaw control in cruising flight. (USAF via Interavia)

type is described as resembling the Shuttle Orbiter or the Lockheed L-2000 supersonic transport design, with a double-delta wing. The inboard wing is sharply swept, reducing nose-on RCS, and its long chord means that it can be thick at the root, and smoothly blended into the fuselage. The two small fins are canted inward.

Despite its planform, the Stealth strike fighter is reported to be subsonic. Supersonic speed calls for reheat, and reheat means a strong thermal signature, so the extra speed might be readily sacrificed. The powerplants are two highly modified General Electric F404s, buried in the fuselage (the modifications may extend to a new and larger fan, increasing the engine's bypass ratio, augmenting thrust and cooling the exhaust). The inlets and exhausts are above the fuselage, and the exhaust is shielded between the twin vertical tails. The pilot sits under a frameless bubble hood, plated with gold or some equally conductive metal. All weapons are carried internally, and the weapon bays can presumably double as sensor bays for the reconnaissance mission, just as the SR-71 sensor bays were originally designed to carry weapons.

The Lockheed aircraft is probably in the 35,000-40,000 pound class, fully loaded. This is less than the maximum weight of an F-4, but the Stealth does not carry a large external load. It may use limited reheat for take-off, but two refanned F404s would provide enough thrust in the cruise. While the aircraft is usually called the Stealth fighter, it is a fighter in the same sense as the F-111. No reports have suggested that the aircraft has an air-to-air role, or any other mission that would call for high-energy-maneuvering flight.

It had been generally assumed that the Stealth fighter would be a smoothly curved shape, but latest reports suggest that though the design has no continuous straight lines or large flat planes, neither does it have any real curves, at least in its body. Instead, the external shape is made up of many small flat planes and straight edges.

This strange shape may be best visualized by a description of an aircraft's radar image contained in one unclassified textbook: like a porcupine, with strong radar reflections as quills. "Don't have any quills pointing toward the radar," the textbook advises. If the flat planes in the Stealth fighter's shape are all aligned in different directions, each of them represents a quill on a different bearing. But because the reflection of any incoming signal is so carefully split up, none of the quills would be long; the aircraft's radar image would be "hairy" rather than quilled.

As was noted in the discussion of Stealth design, even small flat planes have a relatively large RCS. Also, all radar reflections produce side lobes, which may be detectable even if the strong reflections are deflected away from the transmitter. However, this applies only as long as the plane surface is a reflector. The use of the right kind of RAM can redirect the main reflection, to some extent, and can suppress side lobes by absorption. The reported shape of the XST would generate many significant side lobes if it was made in metal, which suggests that the entire airframe is skinned in advanced, Lockheed-developed RAM.

This approach to Stealth apparently dictates extreme precision in assembly. The goal is the complete elimination of electromagnetic and physical discontinuities in the skin. The RAM panels are bonded together and to the substructure, and special nonmetallic fasteners are used for access panels. For these reasons, the aircraft is expensive to build.

Another point about this technique is that the body scatters energy randomly and equally in all directions. A smoothly curved shape may not reflect main lobes toward the transmitter, but may well glint strongly in another direction. It could, therefore, be vulnerable to detection by bistatic radar. The Lockheed-type profile would be as well protected against bistatic radar as it is against a conventional system.

The designation CSIRS (Covert, Survivable, In-weather Reconnaissance/Strike) has been quoted for the aircraft. The meaning of "covert" in this case is very specific: It means that the system must be able to operate without being observed. The U-2 was not a covert system in this sense because it had to operate from overseas bases which were less secure than Groom Lake. Its operations and flight times were easy to observe. The A-12 was different. It was designed with air-refueling capability and global range, and its landings and take-offs could be confined to the continental United States. In the case of the Stealth strike aircraft, a different method is used, because the aircraft is too small for a long unrefueled range and—an interesting point—the standard type of refueling receptacle has a very high RCS. However, since the days of the A-12 the USAF has introduced the giant C-5 freighter, which is large enough to swallow a moderate-sized fighter with folded wings. The C-5 is familiar enough at most USAF bases to attract little attention, and it can carry an aircraft (probably in a portable shelter or container), a ground crew, spares and support equipment. The Stealth aircraft can be ferried securely to an overseas USAF base from which it can reach its objective without refueling.

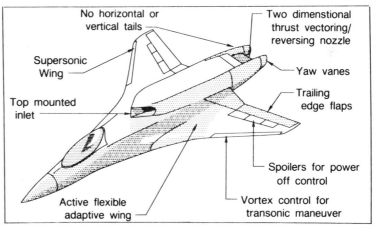

Another Stealth fighter study shows how vertical fins, horizontal stabilizers and canards could be completely eliminated from a future fighter by using a two-dimensional nozzle. The exhaust flaps provide control in pitch, while small yaw vanes attached to the rear of the nozzle replace the rudders. Spoilers and flaps are used for low-speed, low-power control. (Pratt & Whitney)

"In-weather" is another interesting term. The Stealth fighter is presumably designed to operate at night. However, effective in-weather operations imply conditions where cloud and rain would obscure the objective from known passive sensors. This capability calls for some kind of quiet radar, with a very low probability of interception, for reconnaissance and weapon targeting. This would be an expensive piece of equipment, including its low-RCS installation.

If the Stealth technology has been effective, the type should not need to operate at treetop height. The fact that the inlets are on top suggests that security against radar detection from below is important. The advantages of medium-altitude operation include a longer range for reconnaissance sensors, elimination of telltale terrain sensors and a longer mission radius because the aircraft is not constantly maneuvering at low level.

What sort of missions are proposed for the Stealth fighter? The type complements conventional tactical aircraft, with their heavier weapon loads and air-to-air capability, rather than being a replacement or a rival for aircraft such as the F-15 and F-16. Reconnaissance, securing electronic, photographic and (at night) high-quality infrared intelligence on targets and defensive systems, is one mission for the Stealth aircraft. If the aircraft could be operated covertly over hostile territory in peacetime, the sort of electronic surprise that caused problems in the 1973 Middle East war could be avoided. While stand-off systems can detect electronic emissions quite effectively, it takes a close-in reconnaissance flight to correlate such data with the physical appearance of the system.

A Stealth fighter has a natural application in defense suppression. SAMs present a formidable threat to a fighter, but at the same time they are ideal targets: electronically and thermally conspicuous, slow-moving and soft. The Stealth fighter's effectiveness against the SAM is based on the facts that the SAM's surveillance and tracking radars are designed to pick up normal-sized targets just before they enter the system's lethal envelope, and that all SAM systems have a minimum range (due to the time that the missile takes to launch and accelerate) within which they cannot engage a target. Bigger, longer-range SAMs generally have a greater minimum range as well. By the time the radar picks up the small target represented by the Stealth fighter, the attacker may be inside the minimum launch range.

SAMs work because their powerful radars can track an airborne target before the target's own sensors can accomplish the more difficult task of pinpointing the SAM among the clutter of objects on the ground. But the pilot of a Stealth fighter will be able to observe a SAM system by its electronic emissions long before its operators can see him, and will have time to aim a precise strike, with stand-off weapons such as the Hughes AGM-65 Maverick missile, against key components of the system such as its radar and control vehicle. A small number of Stealth strike aircraft could thus eliminate a large number of SAM systems in a very short time, clearing a corridor through the SAM belt for conventional strike aircraft.

The ability to strike targets covertly has some interesting ramifications. A great many countries still rely on a few defense facilities—air bases, long-range SAM sites, medium-range missiles—to threaten their neighbors. Stealth provides the means to eliminate such targets from a medium-altitude, high-accuracy strike without causing civilian casualties and without leaving any recognizable traces.

A number of XST prototypes were tested under the Have Blue program. As well as undergoing flight trials (performance, handling, systems and weapon release), the aircraft were tested against simulated and real Soviet SAM radars. Surveillance and tracking radars from SA-2, SA-3 and SA-6 systems had been captured by Israel from Egyptian forces during the October 1973 war and some had been transferred to the USA in partial payment for the military aid which had proved vital to Israel.

At least two of the XST prototypes were lost during the program. One was reported to have broken up in flight in 1979, injuring pilot Bill Parks, and another crashed after an equipment failure in April 1982. Before the second accident, however, the decision to produce an operational version of the aircraft in quantity had been made.

By 1979, it was clear that the Stealth concept was meeting Lockheed's claims. The Carter administration, approaching the 1980 presidential election and vulnerable to "soft on defense" charges, made some unspecific revelations about Stealth technology in August 1980. Apart from emphasizing that much more money was being put into Stealth projects, the statements revealed nothing, but that did not save the jinxed

Lockheed's Stealth fighter is reported to be a tailless double-delta design, operating at subsonic speed. The Maverick, shown here, is a very likely weapon for the type. Once its video or IR sensor has been aimed at a target, it homes in automatically, requiring no command signals and putting out no electronic emissions, and it cannot be jammed or deceived. The Stealth fighter can use such a weapon very effectively, because it can survive at higher altitudes than can a conventional aircraft. It can therefore aim the missile at greater range, and the missile itself will fly farther. (Michael A. Badrocke)

administration. Opponents said that the announcement jeopardized national security in the interests of party politics.

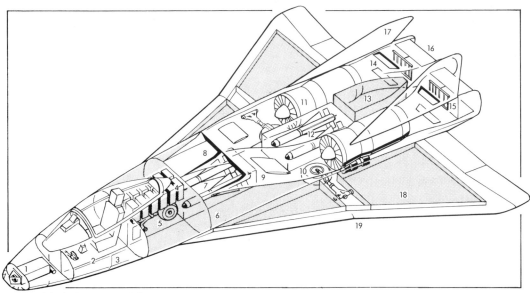

Some likely features of the enigmatic Lockheed Stealth strike fighter are shown in this view. The powerplant, fuel and weapons are all enclosed within the fuselage. The inlets are submerged in the upper surface of the body. The engines may use limited afterburning for take-off, but not in combat. (Michael A. Badrocke)

KEY
 1 *Forward-looking infrared (FLIR) and laser rangefinder, in retractable pod*
 2 *Bays for palletized optical and electronic reconnaissance equipment*
 3 *Fuselage skinned in small, perfectly flat panels of RAM*
 4 *Shielded bay for navigation and flight control electronics*
 5 *Nose-wheel bay*
 6 *Fuselage fuel tanks*
 7 *Forward weapon bay for two AGM-65 Maverick air-to-surface missiles*
 8 *Semisubmerged dorsal air inlet*
 9 *Curved inlet duct, with absorbent walls and baffles*
10 *Main landing gear*
11 *Modified GE F404 engine with new fan and increased bypass ratio*
12 *Aft weapon bay for two AGM-65s*
13 *Rear fuselage fuel tank*
14 *Auxiliary air inlets to reduce exhaust temperature and IR signature*
15 *Absorbent carbon-carbon baffles in exhaust*
16 *Two-dimensional, absorbent exhaust nozzles*
17 *All-moving, all-composite fins with no metal parts*
18 *Wing fuel tanks*
19 *Extensive deep-section RAM on leading and trailing edges*

Production of the Stealth fighter was authorized in 1981. How many aircraft are involved is a matter for rumor and speculation. However, Wall Street analysis of Lockheed's financial results, together with the employment totals at Burbank, suggests that the program is large. The production program appears to involve as many people as the A-12/SR-71 project at its peak. During that time, a maximum of 10,000 Lockheed people built eight of the large and complex aircraft per year. The Stealth aircraft is much smaller and less difficult to build; although the production rate will be nothing

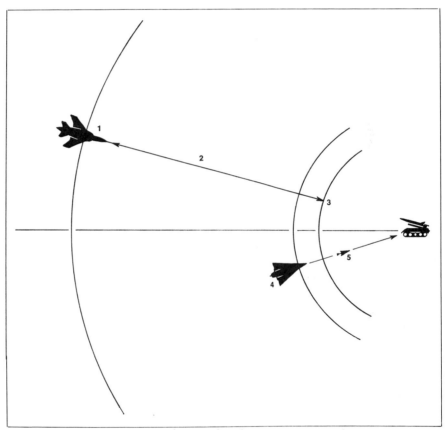

SAM systems are designed to detect conventional targets (1) in time to identify them, slew and elevate the launcher, prepare the missile and fire as the target approaches the system (2). However, all SAM systems have a minimum range (3) determined by the reaction time of the system and the acceleration and maneuvering capability of the missile. Against a Stealth aircraft, the detection range (4) may be very close to the minimum range, and the attacker may be close enough to launch a Maverick missile. In this way, the SAM's main tactical advantage (the ability to fire at the aircraft before the aircraft can shoot back) is eliminated.

like that attained by a similar number of people building conventional fighters, it will be higher than that of the SR-71. Estimates range from eight to sixty aircraft per year. Given that the aircraft is specialized, expensive and global in concept and capability, the higher estimate is probably too high. The lower estimate does not tie in with the workforce figures and the size of the aircraft, unless another classified aircraft program is also under way at Burbank.

Another piece of evidence, however, is a new USAF facility near the northwest corner of the restricted Nellis range, near Tonopah, Nevada. Visible from outside the range, but not mentioned in unclassified documents or maps, the base includes many small hangars as well as the normal large buildings. This is unusual because most military aircraft in the continental United States, particularly in the Sunbelt, are parked outdoors—with the exception of secure types such as the SR-71. The Tonopah base is rumored to be the operating base for the Lockheed Stealth aircraft, which is not unlikely. There has been no report that the aircraft have been permanently located at any open base, while deliveries have undoubtedly started and it is unlikely that Groom Lake could accommodate both flight-test and service operations.

Making the very large assumption that the Tonopah base has been built to house the Stealth aircraft, it is possible to guess at some likely deployment figures. One base would accommodate one wing with a nominal strength of 72 operational aircraft. Taking losses, maintenance, training and special test aircraft into account, this would imply a production run of 120 aircraft, and probably a production rate of fifteen to twenty aircraft per year. Between forty and sixty of the aircraft would have been in service by mid-1985.

The designation of the aircraft is not known. For some time, the aircraft was thought to be designated F-19, because no aircraft had been publicly announced between the F-18 Hornet and the F-20 Tigershark. More recently, however, the USAF has flatly denied that the designation F-19 had been assigned, maintaining that it was deliberately omitted to avoid confusion with the MiG-19. Then, in 1985, the Department of Defense assigned the designation F-21A to the IAI Kfir, although the potential for confusion with the MiG-21 would seem much greater. The USAF said that the policy of avoiding the numbers used by Soviet aircraft had changed. In any event, the USAF denies that any F-19s are in the inventory.

For some reason, possibly connected with its design and possibly with its mission, the Lockheed aircraft is more highly classified than the ATB. The USAF at least admits to the existence of the bomber, which is to be produced at an open site. The Stealth program is black even by Skunk Works standards; it has remained under cover much longer than the A-12, which was unveiled within two years of its first flight. For the time being, the aircraft is an enigma.

CHAPTER 5

Stealth bomber

As the operator of the SR-71 fleet and the different reconnaissance drones, Strategic Air Command was an early arrival in the reduced-observability business. Its Advanced Manned Strategic Aircraft (AMSA) requirement, issued in 1965, was one of the first mainstream aircraft specifications to put a strong emphasis on RCS reduction, as was apparent in the winning design, the Rockwell B-1. The blending of wing and body was more marked than on any previous aircraft (the B-1 was designed before the F-16) and the avoidance of flat vertical planes made the aircraft look odd to an aerospace world still used to rectilinear Mach 2 shapes. The engine installation was at least partly influenced by reduced RCS, the inlets being shielded against look-down radar by a large-area glove. However, it was also one of the few acceptably efficient and structurally practical layouts for a large variable-sweep aircraft. Other features of the design—such as the stabilizer, forming a right-angle with the vertical fin—were less conducive to low RCS.

Primarily, though, the B-1 was designed to confound ground-based radars by operating at low altitude, and by using an extremely powerful integrated jamming system and an advanced decoy. It was the advanced decoy system that almost proved the bomber's undoing. The potential of Boeing's ADM-86 SCAD (Subsonic Cruise Armed Decoy) was so great that it began to be developed as a weapon in its own right. In 1977, the Carter administration found it possible to cancel the B-1 production program in favor of a system based on the decoy's descendant, the AGM-86 Air-Launched Cruise Missile (ALCM).

Although plans to build 240-plus B-1A bombers had been canceled, the possibility of developing a new bomber was not ruled out, and B-1 flight development was permitted to continue. This included a long series of "bomber penetrativity evaluation" tests, conducted at Nellis AFB in 1979. They produced some remarkable results. At 600 knots, 250 feet above the ground, following a winding track around and over the Nevada mountains, and firing powerful and accurately directed packages of electronic half-truths at any radar close enough to be a problem, the B-1 proved very hard to track. The control centers frequently had no idea where the intruder was until it popped up over the hills on its final attack run. The tests were a big step forward for the manned bomber's advocates.

Studies of new strategic aircraft were funded under the Carter administration, with an emphasis on systems which would be less expensive or better than the B-1.

While SAC's requirement for new equipment remained stable in numbers, several factors had changed since the days of AMSA. The advent of the cruise missile had created a potential need for a heavy-payload aircraft, such as a modified transport, which would launch cruise missiles from outside Soviet airspace. As a result, the "penetrator" mission became more distinct. Meanwhile, the Soviet Union was reorganizing and re-equipping its air defenses, making considerable advances in weapons that would be effective against low-level targets. In the late seventies, US intelligence services observed tests of several new weapons: an improved airborne early-warning and control (AEW&C) aircraft, capable of tracking a low-flying target against ground clutter; fighters with look-down/shoot-down radar and missile systems, capable of engaging low-flying aircraft; high-power, jamming-resistant monopulse ground radars; and a large, expensive and advanced SAM, called the SA-10.

Another major influence on the emerging requirement was the evident and demonstrated success of the Stealth concept for ultra-low-observables aircraft. By 1979, SAC no longer had the resurrection of the B-1 as a high priority, although Rockwell continued to offer simplified, lower-cost versions of the design, some of them with fixed wings. Instead, SAC was looking at a relatively inexpensive, stop-gap penetrator proposed by General Dynamics, based on existing F-111 airframes. Under

North American's XB-70 Valkyrie was intended to replace the B-52, but production plans were canceled before the purely experimental prototypes flew. One reason was that its size and its design—with enormous air intakes and many right angles and slab surfaces—made it readily detectable on radar. (Rockwell)

this force plan, advocated by SAC in 1979-80, the B-52s would be used to launch cruise missiles, and a new advanced bomber using Stealth technology would be developed to replace the General Dynamics aircraft, the FB-111H, in the nineties. Under a program called Saber Penetrator, design studies for a Stealth bomber were commissioned in the late seventies.

Bomber development was one of the first major military-technical decisions to face the Reagan administration, elected in November 1980. Having vocally criticized the decision to cancel B-1 production, the new team was committed to launching a new bomber program. There was a difference of opinion between SAC and the USAF headquarters on the best approach to take to the requirement. Both were firm in the view that the Stealth bomber was the best long-term choice for the penetrator role, but that the B-52H, SAC's best in-service penetrating bomber, would be outclassed by Soviet defenses before the new aircraft could be ready. However, while SAC considered the FB-111H acceptable as an interim penetrator, stating that 155 FB-111Hs were equal to 100 B-1s, the USAF command decided to ask for both a resurrected B-1, incorporating some Stealth technology, and a Stealth bomber. Eventually, the USAF program was authorized.

There were several reasons for the apparently extravagant decision to build two bombers rather than taking the much more economical course of building twice as many aircraft of a single type. Some of the reasons were good, some indifferent, and

Stealth features were evident in the design of the original Rockwell B-1, with its wing-to-body blending and inlets concealed under the inner wing. (Rockwell)

some bad. The worst reason, undoubtedly, was that Ronald Reagan had severely criticized Jimmy Carter's cancellation of the B-1, so the Reagan administration was reluctant to endorse that decision.

The USAF headquarters command had an indifferent reason for not joining SAC in support of the FB-111H. It was not a good reason, but it was politically sound. By 1985, a new administration might be in office, and the Stealth bomber would still be in the early development stage and vulnerable to the ax. Either the B-1 or the FB-111H would be well advanced in development and production, and less likely to be canceled. In that event, though, the B-1 would be far more useful to the USAF than the stop-gap FB-111H; it would be more capable, it would have far more capacity for future development and—a very important factor—it would still be in production, while the FB-111H was confined to a limited number of existing airframes.

Better reasons for a two-bomber program included the technical risks inherent in the Stealth concept, and the fact that implicit competition between the two programs would keep both teams on their toes. The B-1 was also more of a known quantity than the FB-111H, which was so extensively reworked that it was almost a new airplane. Finally, the existence of the B-1 might make it possible for the Stealth aircraft to be

One of the reasons for the cancellation of the B-1A was the fact that it would have been vulnerable to new weapons such as the SA-10 missile shown here, even with a much lower RCS than the B-52. (US Department of Defense)

more effective because more time could be allowed for development, and the Stealth aircraft would not need to be compromised for the heavy-payload missions, such as carrying cruise missiles or conventional bombs.

Some months before the decision was officially announced, it was clear that a new Stealth bomber would be ordered; the choice lay between the Stealth bomber alone, or the Stealth and the B-1. Lockheed and Rockwell were teamed to develop a Stealth bomber, and seemed unstoppable. Lockheed had practically invented Stealth, Rockwell had built the B-1, and the two companies had a virtual monopoly of US experience in large, modern combat aircraft.

Enter Northrop Corporation, better known as a manufacturer of lightweight fighters, and Boeing, which had not flown a new combat aircraft since 1952. The two companies had joined forces on a new bomber design, based on an old concept: Northrop's Flying Wing, extensively tested in the forties but passed over by the USAF in favor of more conventional aircraft.

As its name suggests, the Flying Wing has no tail and no fuselage. All the elements of the aircraft—engines, warload, crew, systems and fuel—are housed within an oversized wing. The basic advantage of the Wing, as conceived by designer and company founder Jack Northrop, is that all the weight of the aircraft is spread along the span so that the weight is where the lift is. This is not the case in a conventional aircraft.

A number of changes were incorporated in the B-1B to reduce RCS. The front faces of the inlets were swept back, and the inlets were heavily treated with RAM and fitted with internal baffles. The structure around the swinging wing was completely redesigned to eliminate the large cavity which, on the B-1A, opened up when the wing was moved forward, and RAM was added to the airframe. (Rockwell)

In the late seventies, Boeing studied this all-wing bomber with tiny ventral rudders and flush inlets. Stability and control would present a challenge for this aircraft, designed for development in the nineties. Boeing is a major subcontractor on the Advanced Technology Bomber program. (Boeing)

This Boeing study represents a more conservative approach, with a conventional fuselage and separate tail surfaces. The V tail is a promising feature for a Stealth type because its surfaces are highly oblique to the incoming signal at most observation angles. (Boeing)

Most of the weight is in the middle, so the wing is under tremendous bending forces. On a properly designed Flying Wing, these forces are much smaller, so the wing can have a very large span—which is aerodynamically efficient—without becoming unacceptably heavy. At the same time, the "parasite drag" of the fuselage is eliminated.

The design of the Flying Wing had reached a high level of refinement by the time the program ended in early 1951. The 172-foot-span, piston-engined XB-35 and the jet-powered YB-49 had demonstrated acceptable handling without vertical rudders, and featured excellent payload and range performance. A number of factors accounted for the decision not to produce the aircraft in quantity. The B-35 suffered problems with its engine installation, and by the time these were solved the USAF was no longer interested in a new piston-engined bomber. The YB-49, on the other hand, was limited in speed by the use of the B-35 airframe, and the contemporary Boeing B-47 was much faster. Another problem was that the airframe had been designed in the period 1941-42, before the development of nuclear weapons. It carried its bomb load in eight small bays, none large enough for a nuclear weapon. A complete structural redesign would have been necessary to carry one of the large nuclear weapons in service at that time.

The fact that a Flying Wing is an excellent basis for a Stealth aircraft was apparent not only to Northrop; both Rockwell and Boeing studied such designs in 1979-80. Stealth advantages of an all-wing configuration include the absence of large vertical surfaces and the fact that most of the skin surface is flat and almost horizontal—incoming radar waves tend to be heavily diffracted, an effect that can be heightened with the use of RAM. The large area makes it possible to build deep radar-absorbent structures into the leading and trailing edges, and the depth and chord of the wing provide plenty of space to hide the engines and other equipment.

Another Boeing study emphasized wing-body-nacelle blending, but was otherwise unusually conventional. Note the inward-angled nacelles. (Boeing)

Northrop designers blew the dust off the Flying Wing data and prepared an updated version. Many new technologies, such as fly-by-wire, are particularly beneficial for a Flying Wing. For example, the wingtips of the B-35 had to take the place of the tailplane, providing a downward force to keep the aircraft stable, and this caused extra drag and reduced the Flying Wing's natural efficiency advantage. With fly-by-wire, the aircraft need no longer be naturally stable, so the drag penalty is eliminated. Another useful technique is active load alleviation; this involves deflecting the control surfaces to counter short-period bending loads caused by maneuvering and turbulence, and means that the wing can be less heavily stressed and significantly lighter.

Northrop's associates were also important to the program. Boeing brought its expertise in avionics integration (based on its work on the AWACS and the B-1) and Vought contributed specialized guidance and control systems. General Electric was selected to supply the engines, probably modified versions of the B-1 powerplant, the F101.

In October 1981, the Northrop team was awarded contracts to develop the Advanced Technology Bomber (ATB), and to prepare for the construction of 132 production aircraft. Since then, Northrop has set up a secure facility at Pico Rivera, in

This Rockwell all-wing design, also dating back to the 1979-80 period, features buried engines and small fins under the trailing edge. Spanning only 77 feet, this design was claimed to be capable of carrying twice as much payload as an FB-111. (Rockwell)

the Los Angeles area, to accommodate the engineers on the program, and in early 1985 a production facility for the ATB was under construction at Palmdale. The first aircraft—possibly preceded by a subscale prototype for aerodynamic and RCS testing—will fly in late 1987. If all goes according to plan, the ATB will be in service in 1991 or 1992. The ATB will replace the B-1 as the penetrator element of SAC; the B-1 was due to start replacing the B-52H in that role in late 1985, and will take over the cruise-missile launcher mission from the B-52s as the ATB becomes operational.

It has been reported that the ATB has been scaled up since the start of the program, to the point where it is now nearly the same size as the B-1 and may weigh as much as 400,000 pounds for take-off. However, its payload and range are not as great as those of the more conventional bomber. It reportedly carries a maximum of 40,000 pounds of weapons, while the B-1's normal weapon load is 75,000 pounds and the older bomber can lift even greater loads on a conventional bombing mission. One reason for the difference could be that the ATB is designed to accomplish its mission

Northrop's Advanced Technology Bomber is thought to bear a remarkable resemblance to the Northrop YB-49, one of a series of all-wing bomber and reconnaissance aircraft tested by the USAF in 1948-52. Even with the primitive stability-augmentation systems of the day, the YB-49 flew without movable rudders, and with very small vertical fins. A small silhouette was claimed as a tactical advantage for the type, at a time when many fighters still needed to make a final interception by human eyesight. (Northrop)

without refueling. Apart from the difficulty of making a refueling receptable Stealthy, a refueling rendezvous with a non-Stealthy tanker could give the bomber's position away. Another influence on the payload is that the penetrating bomber is primarily armed with thermonuclear free-fall weapons, which have a greater yield in proportion to their weight than do cruise missiles.

The ATB will have a far smaller RCS than the B-1B, drastically reducing the effective range of every Soviet radar, including that of the Ilyushin Mainstay AEW&C aircraft. The result is that far more radar systems, including the expensive Mainstays, will be needed to maintain coverage around the perimeter of the Soviet Union. The ATB, too, will probably be able to detect the Mainstay radar long before it is detected itself, and can maneuver to reduce the chance of detection. The ATB should also be able to penetrate at medium or high altitude, giving it one important advantage: Its sensors will be able to "see" much farther than those of the low-flying B-1. For this reason, the ATB is being touted as the answer to mobile intercontinental missile systems such as the SS-X-24. The ATB's offensive systems may include laser radar and an automatic target recognizer, a very fast computer which scans the laser radar return for the characteristic signatures of targets.

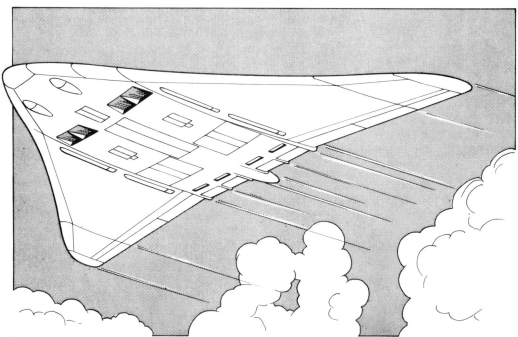

The ATB may look much like this: a very large all-wing aircraft, with a span of around 180 feet. Such a large aircraft can easily accommodate some effective radar-absorbent structure, and the all-wing layout makes it possible to bury the engines deep inside the airframe. (Michael A. Badrocke)

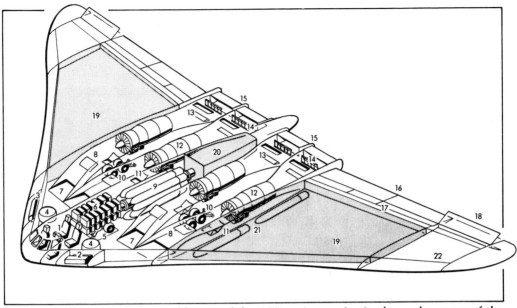

Internal layout of the ATB, as I conceive it, shows that most of the center-section is likely to be taken up by the engines, crew station and weapons bay. Concealing the engines effectively, while ensuring that they operate efficiently, is one of the challenges facing the designer of a Stealth aircraft. (Michael A. Badrocke)

KEY

 1 Four-man crew
 2 Covert strike radar
 3 Electronic warfare antennae
 4 Retractable packs for FLIR and laser radar systems
 5 Nose-wheel bay
 6 Shielded avionics bay
 7 Completely flush ventral inlets
 8 Serpentine, RAM-treated duct with internal streamwise baffles
 9 Common Strategic Rotary Launcher (eight cruise missiles or B83 thermonuclear gravity weapons)
10 Main landing gear
11 Auxiliary air inlets
12 Four modified General Electric F101 engines
13 Auxiliary inlets for IR suppression
14 Absorbent baffles for IR and radar suppression
15 Two-dimensional vectoring/reversing nozzles
16 Flaperons, possibly with flexible covering
17 Roll/lift-dump spoilers
18 Split wing-tip surfaces function as elevators, rudders and air brakes
19 Wing fuel tanks
20 Fuselage fuel tank
21 Possible conformal carriage of Advanced Cruise Missiles
22 External RAM

Thermal signature is probably a bigger problem for the ATB than for a tactical fighter. The aircraft is larger, and it operates in a less cluttered environment, where the defenders can use large high-resolution IR systems without being swamped with targets. New methods of signature control will have to be developed, particularly in view of the long background of Soviet research into IR detection.

The ATB exemplifies some of the ways in which Stealth compounds the problems of a defensive system, although such a large aircraft, operating in hostile airspace, will probably not be completely immune to detection by radar. However, the ATB will use electronic countermeasures (ECM) or jamming equipment, also developed by Northrop, to prevent hostile radars from tracking the target.

Stealth multiplies the effectiveness of ECM. Because the target is smaller, less power need be used to create a false return that masks the true one. There are also a number of attractive ECM techniques that have been developed in laboratories over the years, but were shelved because they required too much power. Now that the target to be masked is smaller, some of these have become practical, so an adversary has to counter more different types of jamming as well as the more effective use of traditional techniques.

Another problem for the defender is that the systems needed to detect a Stealth aircraft, such as very large, long-wavelength early-warning radars, are by no means the same as those needed to catch a B-1—and both types of system must be maintained in service as long as the adversary has both low-altitude and Stealth systems. At the same time, the power being emitted by the counter-B-1 systems will be rapidly intercepted by the high-flying Stealth aircraft. Using a secure, low-side-lobe, extremely high frequency (EHF) link, the Stealth aircraft could transmit the information, via satellite, to incoming B-1s.

The future of the ATB is becoming more certain. Production will not be authorized before the aircraft flies; Rockwell and Lockheed are proposing a version of the B-1 with additional RAM and other changes to reduce its RCS and improve its ability to penetrate. The proposal has its attractions, although such an aircraft would not be as Stealthy as the ATB.

Estimates suggest that the ATB program will cost $47 billion in current prices, so that each aircraft will cost $350 million, compared with $270 million (on a fixed-price contract) for the B-1. Some estimates of the ATB cost are even higher, ranging up to almost $500 million per aircraft, while the price of a new B-1C could be less than the B-1B cost, which includes research and development. The current B-1B production program is due to end abruptly in 1988, an election year. However, it seemed in late 1985 that the original two-bomber plan was safe, and that B-1 production was not to be extended.

Meanwhile, the ATB remains at the pinnacle of aerospace technology—an aircraft designed to penetrate the world's sophisticated air defense system, at high altitude, and pass undetected. There can be few bigger design challenges.

CHAPTER 6

Vanishing air force

The Stealth bomber and the Stealth fighter are only two of many programs aimed at developing less detectable weapons. From now on, virtually any aircraft designed to go into battle will use reduced observables to a greater or lesser extent. It is important, though, to distinguish between weapons that use reduced observables as one of a number of ways to complete the missions and survive, and true Stealth systems which rely mainly on avoiding detection.

This trend to reduce observability is apparent in modified versions of existing aircraft, such as the B-1B and the General Dynamics F-16F. The latter is a particularly good example. It has a markedly lower RCS than the original F-16, thanks to its more slender fuselage, its longer intake duct, greater leading-edge sweep and lack of stabilizers and ventral fins. (In late 1985, unfortunately, it appeared unlikely to see production in the near future, because of funding constraints.)

Also falling into the reduced-observables category are the composite-fuselage helicopters being developed by Bell and Sikorsky for the US Army under the Advanced Composite Airframe Program (ACAP) project. The angled fuselage sides of these aircraft are intended to eliminate the large flat-plate area of the conventional helicopter, and to help defeat radar-guided gun systems. Such technology will be incorporated in the forthcoming Light Helicopter Experimental (LHX) scout and transport helicopter.

Another class of vehicle to exploit reduced observables is the reconnaissance drone. These vehicles have undergone a dramatic change since the days of the Lightning Bugs. The typical reconnaissance drone is now a tiny machine, like an overgrown version of an enthusiast's flying model. This is no coincidence, because it was aeromodellers who first put new, lightweight cameras on their models and invented a new class of weapon.

Lockheed's all-wing Aquila, being developed for the US Army, carries low observables much further than most reconnaissance drones, but most of them make some use of RAM and design features to avoid detection. However, the aircraft are so small to begin with that the task does not involve highly advanced Stealth technology.

One important and advanced Stealth system is the Advanced Cruise Missile (ACM) under development by General Dynamics. The ACM was designed to supplement, and eventually replace, the current Boeing ALCM. The ALCM is not a large target, but it is certainly bigger than it needs to be, with its dorsal ram inlet, and it is

An example of how some Stealth characteristics can be built into an existing design is the General Dynamics F-16XL prototype (above). It has a lower RCS than the standard F-16C, (top) for a number of reasons. The arrow-winged XL is more slender; it has no separate stabilizer and no ventral fins; its leading edges are more sharply swept; it has a longer inlet duct, and its weapons are partly concealed beneath the wing. (General Dynamics)

potentially vulnerable to detection and interception. As well as being Stealthy, the ACM is intended to be more accurate and to have a much greater range than the existing ALCM, enabling the launcher aircraft to stand off outside the range of MiG-31 interceptors or of the new supersonic-cruise long-range interceptor which the Soviet Union is believed to be developing.

The General Dynamics missile will resemble the ALCM in size, because it is designed to fit the same launcher. It is likely to feature a ventral air inlet and a shielded exhaust nozzle. It will also use a different guidance system which, unlike that of the ALCM, does not rely on radar altimeter transmissions to update the inertial platform—laser radar systems developed by Hughes and McDonnell Douglas are to be tested in support of the program. The ACM will also use new fuels and the more advanced Williams F112 engine to give it a longer range than the Boeing weapon. It will probably enter service late in the eighties.

Another important program in which Stealth plays a major role is the Advanced Tactical Fighter (ATF), intended to enter service in the mid-nineties. The ATF is more than just a Stealth aircraft; it is also designed to use short runways, and to sustain supersonic speeds much longer than current aircraft. However, the USAF wants the design to be as Stealthy as possible within certain performance, weight and cost targets.

This is because the latest Soviet fighters (which will form the majority of the ATF's opponents) reflect the philosophy of the F-15. The new Mikoyan MiG-29 and Sukhoi Su-27 are believed to carry large, powerful radars and long-range, radar-guided mis-

This Rockwell design, representing the company's early thoughts on the USAF's Advanced Tactical Fighter requirement, shows a great deal of Stealth influence. In particular, the broad center-section and highly blended configuration make the aircraft seem to be a flying wing, with the addition of a nose and engine nacelles. (Rockwell)

siles, and their airframes have clearly not been designed with low RCS as a high priority. The Soviets apparently intend to use radar and missile improvements to achieve a "first-look, first-shot" advantage over their opponents.

Stealth technology is incorporated in the ATF to turn this development into a handicap. The range at which the Soviet fighters can detect and track a target and guide missiles will be reduced. The ATF's own detection systems are heavily biased toward passive methods. Its EW system will be designed to pick up hostile emitters over a wide waveband, and to locate and identify them accurately. Its radar will have passive modes for more accurate emitter tracking, and it may carry dual-mode missiles which home in on electronic emissions at long ranges, and use all-aspect IR homing for the final interception. With this system, an enemy's powerful radar, intended to give first sight of the opponent, will do precisely the opposite.

One of the challenges in the ATF program will be combining Stealth with high performance, low production and maintenance costs, and other normal fighter requirements. The program is expected to lead to new developments in wideband, reasonably priced RAM with good structural qualities.

Another active USAF requirement is for a stand-off "sensor platform," a high-altitude, subsonic Stealth aircraft designed to carry advanced electronic intelligence systems and the Joint Stars radar, being developed to track individual ground targets hundreds of miles away.

ATF technology will also be available for the US Navy's next combat type, the Advanced Tactical Aircraft (ATA). However, the USN has decided to meet its needs through most of the nineties with updated versions of the F-14 fighter and A-6 attack aircraft. The ATA will not be needed much before the year 2000, and its definition is at a

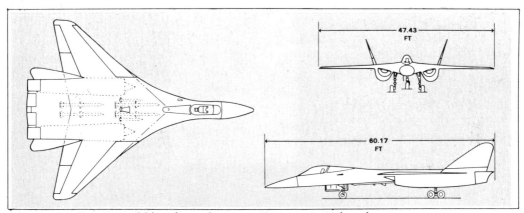

The Rockwell ATF would be about the same size as an F-15, but the new fighter is expected to have an RCS 100 times smaller than the current service type. Note the blended nacelles and the half-cone inlets, which make it easier to conceal the engine faces from view. Weapons are recessed into the underside of the body, between the inlet ducts, reducing both drag and RCS. (Rockwell)

very early stage. Meanwhile, it is possible that some US Navy missions will be performed by versions of the USAF's Lockheed Stealth fighter, in the same way that USAF U-2s operate from aircraft carriers from time to time.

Other Stealth programs are so effectively classified that virtually nothing is known about them. The number, size and importance of black programs are seldom appreciated. Lockheed, for example, was known in early 1985 to be working on four black programs, each valued in excess of $1 billion. One of them was the Stealth strike fighter; another was the new KH-12 Shuttle-launched spy satellite. The third program may have been a Stealth cruise missile for the US Navy, designed to be launched from Navy attack aircraft against heavily defended targets such as Soviet air bases and

Lockheed's ATF study (to be submitted to the USAF in late 1985) may resemble this impression issued by the company, although some details have undoubtedly been omitted or changed for reasons of security. It is externally conventional, but would incorporate a great deal of the sophisticated RAM technology developed for the Stealth fighter. Note the careful integration of the canard foreplane into the fuselage chine, avoiding any acute corners, and the simple, bluff shapes of the fuselage section, and the rounded exhaust nozzle fairings. (Lockheed)

Another view of the Lockheed ATF design shows its simple shape and the two-dimensional exhaust nozzles. Note the auxiliary doors ahead of the main nozzles. Similar doors were incorporated on the Stealth fighter drawing before this Lockheed impression was released. (Lockheed)

warships. The existence of this system has been reported since 1980. Lockheed was also developing a Stealth cruise missile for the USAF, but this program was terminated in favor of the General Dynamics weapon. As for the fourth project, no analyst will even hazard a guess. It may be the mysterious Aurora aircraft, the existence of which was inadvertently revealed in the Pentagon's 1985 budget request. Some $455 million was requested for Aurora production, to be spent in 1987.

No reasonable person can believe that the other US warplane suppliers are not deeply engaged in Stealth research. Certainly, some of them have flown or plan to fly Stealth prototypes, to demonstrate technology for their ATF proposals and other future programs. Building such a demonstrator is costly, but if it is done in the right way, in a Skunk Works type of organization, it is affordable. Northrop, for example, spent $775 million on the F-20 program up to 1984, building and flying three prototypes of an operational fighter. A bare-bones technology demonstrator would be consider-

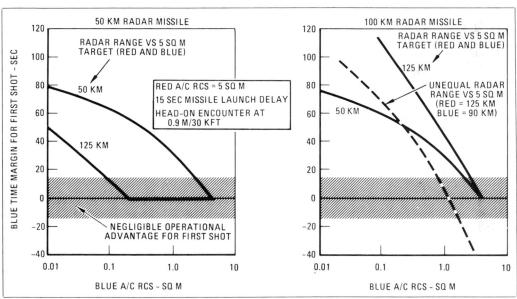

This complex chart is worth a close look. It shows a head-on beyond-visual-range missile engagement between Red, a conventional fighter with a five-square-meter frontal RCS, and Blue, an advanced fighter. The left-hand chart assumes that each fighter carries a missile with a 50 km maximum launch range, and the right-hand chart is based on a missile which can be fired 100 km from the target. If Blue has a frontal RCS under 0.1 square meter, Blue's pilot will see Red first, and may be able to fire 60-80 seconds earlier if the two aircraft have radars of equal power. Even if Red has a slightly more powerful radar (broken line, right-hand chart), it will not compensate for the difference in RCS, and Blue still holds the advantage. The chart is also significant in that it seriously mentions an RCS of 0.01 square meter (similar to that of a bird) for a tactical fighter. (Northrop)

ably less expensive, perhaps costing $75 million to $100 million a year—not much to a giant such as General Dynamics, McDonnell Douglas or Boeing.

There is not much physical or published evidence for any of this activity. The costs are small enough to be untraceable in the annual reports. However, on a recent visit to a small company in California, I noticed some composite airframe components which clearly did not belong to any known aircraft, because no known aircraft of that size—larger than a tactical fighter, judging by the size of the parts—has flaperons and spoilerons. The first reply to queries was "no comment" but the company later said that the components were being built for the Boeing Military Airplane Company. Boeing's response to a further query was, not surprisingly, "no comment." The project may be connected with the "sensor platform mission."

Rumors of other programs are everywhere. So far, however, none of them has elicited more than a flat denial from the USAF or the industry, indicating that they are, at least, sufficiently inaccurate to be denied without falsehood.

Outside the United States, Stealth appears to have received rather less attention, mainly because no other Western nation has the resources to build and operate an entire fleet of specialized Stealth aircraft. The new European Fighter Aircraft (EFA), to be developed by Britain, Germany and Italy, is not likely to be a highly Stealthy design, but is likely to fall into the same bracket as the F-16F. Some design features of the Experimental Aircraft Prototype (EAP), the forerunner of the EFA, show concern for RCS, such as the drooped foreplanes and wide, shallow inlet; others, such as the big,

Lockheed's Aquila mini-remotely piloted vehicle (RPV) is clearly designed with Stealth in mind. Currently, most RPVs rely on small size and composite materials to escape detection, but true Stealth technology may become more important as counter-RPV tactics and systems are developed. (Lockheed)

single vertical fin and the plain round exhaust nozzles, do not. The same can be said of advanced fighter designs being developed in Israel, France and Sweden. One company with an interest in Stealth is Germany's Dornier, which in late 1985 proposed a finless slender-delta Stealth strike aircraft.

The US Navy, in early 1985, made a public prediction that Soviet aircraft and missiles incorporating Stealth technology would enter service by the end of the decade; this is one reason that the passive infrared search and tracking system is considered to be an important part of the F-14D program. The basis for the Navy's projection was not revealed, but it points out one more facet of Stealth: By the very nature of Stealth, its development is likely to escape the eyes of intelligence assets.

The first point to be made in any assessment of Soviet work on Stealth is that the Soviet designers have a long way to go. The Tu-26 Backfire bomber, for instance, has almost everything a Stealth aircraft does not want: a huge vertical fin, slab sides and air inlets the size of subway tunnels. Even Soviet cruise missiles have active terminal homing, which implies the presence of a forward-facing, high-RCS radar dish, and are extremely large.

The unusual nose shape of the Boeing AGM-86B Air-Launched Cruise Missile was designed to reduce the missile's RCS. However, it is still not too hard to detect, and is to be replaced by General Dynamics' classified Advanced Cruise Missile. (Boeing)

The Soviet Union has been making progress in all the technologies that contribute to Stealth: composites, fly-by-wire, computer-aided design and so on. The Antonov An-124 transport, which was unveiled at the 1985 Paris Air Show, incorporated a fly-by-wire system and a considerable amount of composite material. Soviet industry could undoubtedly produce effective RAM; Soviet materials and production technology are excellent. The main reason the Soviet Union will probably lag in the development of Stealth is philosophical. The system by which the Soviet Union designs and builds military aircraft—or anything else, from vacuum cleaners to aircraft carriers—is centrally controlled and hierarchical. In this hierarchy, the role of the aircraft designer is to find solutions to the requirements formulated by the military command. These

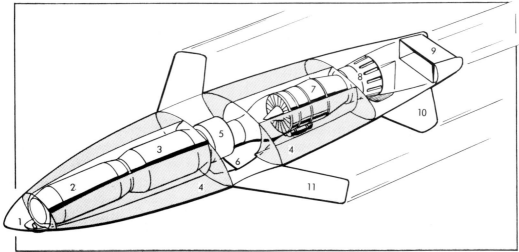

A true Stealth cruise missile should be almost impossible to detect. This impression shows a winged configuration, but such a vehicle could fly by body lift alone; perhaps the wings could be used for efficient cruise, and jettisoned before the final attack run. (Michael A. Badrocke)

KEY
 1 *Laser radar for covert navigation and terrain-following, coupled with automatic target recognition*
 2 *Guidance and avionics package: inertial platform and supercomputer*
 3 *Warhead*
 4 *High-energy boron slurry fuel*
 5 *Active cooling pack matches IR signature of missile to terrain*
 6 *Ventral flush inlet*
 7 *Turbofan engine*
 8 *Exhaust mixer for IR suppression*
 9 *Two-dimensional nozzle for pitch control*
10 *Two all-composite, all-moving ventral rudders*
11 *All-composite wings*

requirements are, inevitably, framed in terms of existing missions, tactics and technology.

The Soviet approach has its advantages, in that it produces systems which come very close to meeting the user's needs (or, rather, the user's perceived needs). However, a requirement drafted at the operational level seldom calls for a radical break with existing ways of tackling a problem because the person who is in charge of writing the requirement is familiar only with existing techniques. Stealth is such a change, and it is unlikely to have originated in the Soviet Union as early as it did in the United States.

Stealth technology will be developed in the Soviet Union when there is a mission for it, but it is hard to say when that will be. The Soviet forces have a different operational philosophy from Western armed forces, and their equipment differs accordingly. The Soviet forces have far more radar-controlled SAMs, and it is these systems that a Stealth fighter such as the Lockheed type is designed to foil. Soviet EW doctrine, too, places a strong emphasis on antiradar weapons and offensive jamming, and the Soviet forces have a heavy investment in this type of equipment; the Stealth concept does not make a good fit with this approach.

It is likely that naval cruise missiles, which are becoming vulnerable to improved shipboard defensive weapons, will be the first candidates for Stealth development in the Soviet Union. Existing weapons in this class are large, and could carry a fair amount of RAM. The first step, however, will be the provision of passive guidance systems. The appearance of improved antishipping missiles will probably be the first indication that Soviet Stealth technology is advancing.

Stealth is going to be an important part of the military balance in the nineties. Leadership in Stealth technology will be a substantial advantage, particularly in air warfare. In the eighteenth century, the German military theoretician Karl von Clausewitz introduced the concept of "the fog of battle," a phrase which sums up all the uncertainty of all observations in action. The advantage of Stealth technology is that it thickens the fog of battle, but—as long as leadership is maintained—it does so for only one side.

Bibliography

Many sources were consulted in the preparation of this book. Some of the most important are listed below.

Technical Papers
Fighter Issues—2000; D. E. Kozlowski, McDonnell Douglas 1981
Future Tactical Strike Fighter Options; Paul V. Bavitz, Grumman 1981
Technology for Quality and Quantity in a new Fighter; Northrop 1981
Development of the SR-71 Blackbird; C. L. Johnson, Lockheed 1982

Books
Radar Cross Section Lectures; A. E. Fuhs, American Institute of Aviation and
    Astronautics 1985
The Lightning Bugs—and other reconnaissance drones; William Wagner, Aero
    Publishers 1985
The Lockheed U-2; Jay Miller, Aerofax 1983
Introduction to Airborne Radar; G. W. Stimson, Hughes Aircraft Company 1984

Periodicals
No book of this kind could be written without extensive browsing and cross-referencing among the pages of the better-informed trade press: *Interavia, IDR, Aviation Week & Space Technology, Defense Week, Air Force Magazine, Armed Forces Journal* and *Flight International.*

Biography

Bill Sweetman is Technical Editor—North America for Interavia SA of Geneva, Switzerland, the publisher of the internationally known *Interavia Aerospace Review* and *International Defense Review.* He has worked on the analysis of secret aircraft programs since the mid-seventies, when he started writing about Soviet aircraft for the British weekly *Flight International.* Bill Sweetman has written more than ten books, including *High-Speed Flight* (Jane's 1983) and *Aircraft 2000* (Hamlyn 1984). A British citizen, he has worked in California since 1981, and lives near San Francisco with his wife, Mary Pat, and sons Martin and Evan.

Index